PRISONS

Inside the Big House

by Andy Hjelmeland

LERNER PUBLICATIONS COMPANY • MINNEAPOLIS

Library of Congress Cataloging-in-Publication Data

Hjelmeland, Andy.
　　Prisons : inside the big house / Andy Hjelmeland.
　　　　p.　cm. — (Pro/Con)
　　Includes bibliographical references (p. 108) and index.
　　Summary: Examines the state and federal prison systems, what
prison life is like in various types of institutions, prison
violence, women in prison, and alternatives to prison.
　　ISBN 0–8225–2607–7 (alk. paper)
　　1. Imprisonment—United States—Juvenile literature. 2. Prisons—
United States—Juvenile literature. [1. Prisons. 2. Prisoners.]
I. Title. II. Series.
HV9471.H58　1996
365'.973—dc20
　　　　　　　　　　　　　　　　　　　　　　　　　　　95–12723

Manufactured in the United States of America
1　2　3　4　5　6　–　S　–　01　00　99　98　97　96

CONTENTS

FOREWORD

If a nation expects to be ignorant and free, . . . it expects what never was and never will be.

Thomas Jefferson

Are you ready to participate in forming the policies of our government? Many issues are very confusing, and it can be difficult to know what to think about them or how to make a decision about them. Sometimes you must gather information about a subject before you can be informed enough to make a decision. Bernard Baruch, a prosperous American financier and an advisor to every president from Woodrow Wilson to Dwight D. Eisenhower, said, "If you can get all the facts, your judgment can be right; if you don't get all the facts, it can't be right."

But gathering information is only one part of the decision-making process. The way you interpret information is influenced by the values you have been taught since infancy—ideas about right and wrong, good and bad. Many of your values are shaped, or at least influenced, by how and where you grow up, by your race, sex, and religion, by how much money your family has. What your parents believe, what they read, and what you read and believe influence your decisions. The values of friends and teachers also affect what you think.

It's always good to listen to the opinions of people around you, but you will often confront contradictory points of view and points of view that are based not on fact, but on myth. John F. Kennedy, the 35th president of the United States, said, "The great enemy of the truth is very often not the lie—deliberate, contrived, and dishonest—but the myth—persistent, persuasive, and unrealistic." Eventually you will have to separate fact from myth and make up your own mind, make your own decisions. Because you are responsible for your decisions, it's important to get as much information as you can. Then your decisions will be the right ones for you.

Making a fair and informed decision can be an exciting process, a chance to examine new ideas and different points of view. You live in a world that changes quickly and sometimes dramatically—a world that offers the opportunity to explore the ever-changing ground between yourself and others. Instead of forming a single, easy, or popular point of view, you might develop a rich and complex vision that offers new alternatives. Explore the many dimensions of an idea. Find kinship among an extensive range of opinions. Only after you've done this should you try to form your own opinions.

After you have formed an opinion about a particular subject, you may believe it is the only right decision. But some people will disagree with you and challenge your beliefs. They are not trying to antagonize you or put you down. They probably believe that they're right as sincerely as you believe you are. Thomas Macaulay, an English historian and author, wrote, "Men are never so likely to settle a question rightly as when they discuss it freely." In a democracy, the free exchange of ideas is not only encouraged, it's vital. Examining and discussing public issues and understanding opposing ideas are desirable and necessary elements of a free nation's ability to govern itself.

The Pro/Con series is designed to explore and examine different points of view on contemporary issues and to help you develop an understanding and appreciation of them. Most importantly, it will help you form your own opinions and make your own honest, informed decision.

Mary Winget
Series Editor

New inmates arrive at a California prison.

INTRODUCTION

The Department of Corrections bus winds its way slowly through the heavy city traffic. An occasional pedestrian glances curiously at the bus, unable to clearly see the shadowy faces obscured by the wire mesh behind the glass windows. The silent occupants of the bus peer out at the street activity—their final glimpse of freedom before prison doors bang shut behind them.

As the bus travels out of the city and into the rolling countryside, 23-year-old Kenny recalls the woman's screams. He stares down at the shackles and chains that bind his arms and legs together. The woman had suddenly appeared in the doorway as he was ransacking the dresser drawers in her bedroom. Their eyes had locked momentarily before he pushed his way past her to escape. She had been an attractive young woman, about his age, pale, and wide-eyed with fear.

"We're home, man," someone says from inside the bus as the prison looms like a medieval fortress—a gray granite structure surrounded by a high concrete wall.

Kenny's mouth is dry, and his heartbeat quickens as the bus pulls up to the stark entrance. He wonders what it will be like inside and asks himself what kind of person he will be after three years behind those walls.

* * *

Sheila hasn't slept well since the burglary. Each time she arrives home now, she hesitates in the doorway before entering, alert for any sign of activity inside. Dreams of the intruder often wake her in the middle of the night—the man coming toward her as she stood screaming in the doorway of her bedroom. She had been sure he would assault or rape her, maybe even murder her. Since that night, every sound frightens her—a door slamming down the hallway, a key turning in a lock in a nearby apartment, a creaking floorboard.

The intruder's face is still clear in her mind, a face no different than that of many young men she passes every day on the street. No mask or gloves to identify him as a burglar. Just a regular-looking guy. What she remembers most from that frozen moment when their eyes met was the indecisive look on his face—as though he wasn't sure whether to flee or . . . who knows what else he might have been thinking?

Police and friends told her how lucky she was that he didn't hurt her. Other victims, they reminded her, hadn't been as fortunate. In the following days and weeks, people advised her to add another lock to her door, carry Mace, install a burglar alarm, get a dog. One fellow at work even suggested that she carry a gun in her purse.

Sheila's behavior and outlook changed. She began paying more attention to stories about crime: the rising crime rate, the shortage of jail and prison space, and the need for more police and tougher laws. Mostly, she felt angry that the man who robbed her had been sentenced to only three years in prison.

* * *

Stories like Sheila's are too common to make the news. Even though statistics show that people are 10 times more likely to be killed in an automobile accident than they are to be murdered, and that the chances of being injured in a home accident are much greater than

An inmate in a maximum-security prison

Many Americans, especially women, hesitate before entering their own homes because they fear the possibility of an intruder.

the chances of being injured in an assault or robbery, many Americans live daily with a fear of crime.

Who are the individuals responsible for creating this pervasive dread—the burglars, assailants, rapists, and murderers? People like Kenny. And when they are caught, what happens to them? Or, more to the point, what *should* happen to them?

Many criminals share one common fate: they end up in prison. Then what? Are they reformed, rehabilitated, transformed into honest members of society? Does the correctional system "correct" or merely churn out more angry and hostile criminals?

The American prison system is a hodgepodge of differing philosophies and environments. Some prisons are extremely harsh while others offer surroundings that are more comfortable than many law-abiding citizens can afford for themselves. A variety of methods are being tried in the United States to reform criminals. Do any of these methods work?

Is it realistic to expect a person to change for the better in a prison environment? Convicted killer Jack Abbott insists, "No one has ever come out of prison a better man."[1] Criminologists (experts on crime) admit that there are no surefire solutions. Rehabilitating criminals is not a science. Some studies have shown that the percentage of repeat offenders is the same no matter what kind of programs inmates undergo. Because criminals do not fit a common mold, what works for some has no effect on others. Some criminals are violent, although most are not. Some are calculatingly clever, while others are borderline retarded. Some are timid sneak thieves; others are bold and intimidating.

With about a million men and women incarcerated in federal and state prisons,[2] the United States locks up more of its citizens than any country in the world.[3] When the prison population is combined with inmates of local jails, juvenile facilities, and those on probation and parole, more than four million Americans are under the jurisdiction of the criminal justice system. This amounts to more than two percent of the entire population of the United States being under correctional supervision. Criminologists and public-finance experts estimate that federal, state, and local governments spent more than $30 billion on corrections in 1994, including building new prisons and expanding existing ones.[4] In addition to the cost of new construction, it costs $12 billion a year to operate existing prisons.[5] In spite of this expansion, nearly every American

Inmates line up in an interior cell at a correctional training facility in Soledad, California.

prison is overcrowded. This overcrowding crisis, combined with the public perception of rising crime rates and disagreement about how criminals should be treated, has stimulated a debate about the role of prisons. Should prisons punish or rehabilitate? Are there cheaper, more effective alternatives to imprisonment? Which prison programs are most successful? What role does education and job training play in turning lives around? Should we abandon the notion that prisons actually reform anyone? Can we afford to keep building prisons at the present rate?

Despite overcrowding, some people contend we don't need additional prisons. Syndicated columnist Neal R. Pierce has repeatedly argued that America's criminal justice system locks up too many people. "We're incarcerating hundreds of thousands of the 'wrong people,'" he claims. "Overwhelmingly, they're guilty of petty crimes and pose no danger to public safety. They're homeless vagrants, petty thieves, bad check passers, people caught with a few ounces of marijuana. And thousands are being held in our jails just because they're too poor to raise bail . . . . Only a quarter of local jail inmates and a third of people held in state prisons are there for violent crimes."[6]

Author Eugene H. Methvin disagrees. He concludes that Americans "are willing to pay the price to lock up criminals for as long as necessary. By building more prisons we can enjoy safe streets and homes again."[7]

Ultimately, what have we learned about crime and criminals in the United States? What is the solution to the crime problem? Or, as more and more people are asking: *Is* there a solution?

A crowded cell block at Folsom Prison in Represa, California

FROM DUNGEONS TO PENITENTIARIES

For most of recorded history, an "eye for an eye" was the most common method of punishing criminals. Citations from the Code of Hammurabi, one of the first legal codes in history, drawn up nearly 4,000 years ago in Babylon, illustrate the ancient view of punishment:

195. If a son strike his father, they shall cut off his fingers.

200. If a man knock out the tooth of another man, they shall knock out his tooth.[1]

The idea that the punishment should fit the crime is also found in the Old Testament: "Eye for eye, tooth for tooth, hand for hand, foot for foot." (Exodus 21:24)

In every age and in nearly every part of the world, the death penalty has been employed as a form of criminal punishment. Only the methods—stoning, hanging, firing squad, beheading (guillotine), electric chair, gas chamber, or lethal injection—differed. For centuries, executions were public events, eagerly attended by the citizenry. A public hanging in England in 1594 offers a graphic example of the death penalty as criminal punishment as well as spectator sport: "While being transported in an open cart to the site of the hanging, three prisoners were jeered at by a howling procession of people. Before they were hanged they were placed in a pillory and pelted with blood, garbage, ordure from the slaughter house, dead cats, turnips, potatoes, rotten eggs. Then, one by one, they were hanged. And while they were still alive, they were cut down and castrated, disembowelled, and quartered."[2]

Torture and mutilation have also been routinely used in punishing criminals. Whipping, branding, confinement in stocks and pillories, cutting off ears and tongues, and boring a hole through the tongue with a hot iron were employed in England and colonial America for minor offenses.

During the Age of Discovery, the maritime powers of Europe established colonies around the globe. Banishment to one of these faraway lands became another way of punishing criminals. England shipped convicts to colonial America and Australia; Spain sent criminals to Hispaniola (the island now occupied by Haiti and the Dominican Republic); Portugal sent most of its criminals to North Africa. The world's best-known penal colony—the infamous Devil's Island—was established by the French off the coast of South America.[3]

Penal colonies required no walls. Prisoners were isolated by miles of ocean in remote areas of the world, often on islands or in tropical jungles. Escape was impossible. Simply staying alive was a daily struggle under the miserable conditions at these far-flung settlements. Convicts routinely succumbed to long days of backbreaking labor, physical abuse, poor food, and disease.

The whipping post and pillory at New Castle, Delaware,
exposed offenders to public scorn and ridicule.

Galley ships were another form of punishment. Dating back to the early Greeks and Romans, these long warships were propelled by oars and sails. Each ship had about 50 oars extending through portholes. Six convicts worked each oar. Slaves, prisoners of war, and criminals were chained below deck to operate the oars.

Imprisonment in ancient and medieval times was primarily used for persons awaiting trial. Dungeons confining only a few prisoners were the earliest forms of imprisonment. Prisons, as we know them, did not exist until the early 1800s.

From the middle 1500s until well into the 1800s, England operated institutions known as "houses of correction," but these were not prisons in the modern sense. They served more as dumping grounds for misfits, debtors, and outcasts than as institutions designed specifically for criminals. Serious criminal offenders were hanged, tortured, banished to penal colonies, or exiled aboard galley ships.

In reaction to the deplorable conditions in England's houses of correction—known also as almshouses, debtors' prisons, houses of charity, and poorhouses—the first reform groups appeared in the latter part of the 18th century. Foremost among these early reformers were the Quakers, members of the Society of Friends. In response to pressure from the Quakers, the English parliament passed a landmark piece of legislation, the Penitentiary Act of 1779. In addition to mandating sanitary and humane conditions within England's various institutions, this bill introduced the new concept of imprisonment, rather than torture or death, as a method of reforming criminals.

Quakers believed that criminals would eventually realize the error of their ways if forced to "meditate" in solitary confinement over their wrongdoings. With only a Bible to read, they would feel penitent (sorry for doing wrong).[4] Influenced by their English counterparts, American Quakers introduced this idea to the United States. The Walnut Street Jail in Philadelphia was one of the earliest correctional facilities to test the new theory of penitence.

In 1829 Pennsylvania opened the Eastern State Penitentiary, setting the standard for America's prisons for the next 150 years. Modeled on Quaker ideas, this maximum-security facility was soon copied by other states. So unique was the idea of rehabilitating criminals that prison reformers from around the world

Eastern State Penitentiary in 1927

Prison administrator and reformer Zebulon Brockway introduced the concept of reduced time for good behavior.

traveled to the United States to study this innovative concept firsthand.

In the 1870s, a prison administrator and reformer named Zebulon Brockway claimed that penitentiaries, with their emphasis on silence and solitude, failed to rehabilitate. He advocated a different approach to reforming criminals—an approach stressing education, athletic events, military drills, and religious instruction. The New York legislature granted Brockway an opportunity to implement his ideas in 1876, when he was appointed superintendent of the Elmira Reformatory. Elmira was for young men between the ages of 16 and 30. Older criminals continued to go to "the pen."[5]

Brockway introduced the concept of *good time*—reduced time in prison for good behavior—as well as *indeterminate sentences* (no set minimum or maximum time). He believed in releasing reformed criminals and keeping incorrigibles (those who cannot or will not reform) indefinitely. Until then, a sentence of one year meant a full 12 months behind bars. (In contrast, now convicts generally have their sentences shortened by one-third if they receive the maximum good-time allowance. Thus, assuming model behavior, prisoners sentenced in today's courts would "max-out" in two years on a three-year term.)

An even earlier release was possible under Brockway's *parole* incentive. Once a prisoner demonstrated that he was reformed, he would be released to serve the remainder of his sentence under supervision. Parole is similar to probation. Under both conditions, people convicted of a crime serve a portion or all of their sentence under the supervision of a parole or probation officer. Probation means the entire prison term is suspended. Under parole, a person serves time in prison but may win early release by showing exemplary behavior and attitude.

Parole and good time are now standard practices in almost all prisons in the United States. Prison administrators have reason to favor these proposals, because inmates are more likely to behave when good behavior means an early release from prison. Opponents of parole, however, maintain it is a mockery of justice for someone sentenced to 10 years, for example, to be released in half that time.

Neither the Quakers' reliance on penitence nor Brockway's creative methods of reforming criminals ever achieved their promise, however, and crime continued to flourish. Meanwhile, penitentiaries became grim bastions of silent convicts marching in lockstep. Except for housing a younger population, reformatories soon resembled penitentiaries in their maximum-security harshness.

Reformers continued fighting for improved prison conditions, but their critics belittled what they saw as misguided attempts to turn prisons into "country clubs." Two men from very different backgrounds agreed that prisons are too easy. Graeme R. Newman, a professor of criminology, stated that "Going to prison should be . . . like descending into hell."[6] J. J. Maloney, who served 13 years in a Missouri penitentiary for murder, would abolish television and radio, job programs, personal belongings in the cell, candy, cigarettes, and most other creature comforts. He would make convicts spend more time in their cells, ensuring that they would do "hard time." [7]

Agitation for prison reform diminished during World War I (1914–1918) and World War II (1941–1945). Many young men (who comprise the majority of prison inmates) were overseas fighting, and the rest of the country was preoccupied with the war effort at home. During the lawless era of Prohibition (1920–1933), few citizens had any sympathy for criminals.

In the late 1940s, following World War II, a new wave of criminologists emerged. Theories that explained criminal behavior as a result of childhood abuse, bad parenting, or a harmful environment became popular. Some criminologists viewed criminals as troubled individuals who could be cured with proper treatment. Other criminologists refused to make such excuses for criminals, pointing out that many Americans regularly overcome deprived childhoods to become law-abiding, successful citizens. Nevertheless, psychologists were installed in most correctional institutions during the 1950s, and treatment and rehabilitation re-

In 1995 Alabama revived the chain gang for repeat offenders who have lost respect for the law.

placed punishment in the effort to reform criminals.

Until the early 1960s, the courts still viewed prisoners as "slaves of the state." Prison wardens were able to run their individual institutions without any outside interference. Inspired by the civil rights movement, prison inmates began petitioning the courts with grievances about inadequate medical care, brutal treatment by guards, bad food, and mail censorship.

With the start of this less stringent view of criminality, prison administrators gradually eliminated the harsher aspects of their institutions. Backbreaking labor (epitomized by the rock pile, where gangs of convicts broke up large rocks with sledgehammers) was discontinued. The silent system and the ball and chain became relics of the past. During the 1950s, 1960s, and

1970s, privileges like watching television and making telephone calls became commonplace. Educational opportunities, including college courses, became available to prisoners. New, smaller prisons were built, which had fences instead of granite or concrete walls.

Despite improved prison conditions, the modern era continues to be plagued by crime. The questions that were being asked 200 years ago are still being asked now. How can we punish without brutalizing? How can we reclaim lives that have gone astray? And how can we solve the social conditions that breed crime?

Prisons are certainly more lenient and humane than in the past. One contributing factor in recent years has been intervention by the courts. A series of court rulings has granted constitutional protection to prisoners. In effect, the U.S. Supreme Court said that the rights guaranteed under the Constitution of the United States did not stop at prison walls. As a result, 41 states are under court order to stop overcrowding and poor delivery of services to inmates under the "cruel and unusual punishment" provision of the Eighth Amendment.[8]

Imprisoned Nation of Islam members, an emerging and militant religious group seeking freedom to practice its religion within prison, have been particularly effective in getting the attention of the courts. Various state courts have issued orders that recognize prison inmates as citizens with certain rights. They are no longer slaves of the state and subject to the whims of the warden.

Several Supreme Court decisions have bolstered the constitutional rights of prisoners. A 1974 decision, *Wolff v. McDonnell,* broke the "hands-off" doctrine, which held that prisoners have no rights and therefore the courts should not intervene.[9] In 1980, a much broader Supreme Court decision—*Civil Rights of Institutionalized Persons*—ruled that virtually all institutionalized persons possess constitutional rights. This decision covered not only prison and jail inmates, but also the mentally ill, disabled, retarded, chronically ill, and handicapped.

Judging from recent developments, however, the pendulum seems to be swinging back to tougher prisons. In 1995, for example, the state of Alabama revived chain gangs. Commissioner Ron Jones believes that prisoners should be less comfortable. Convicts work along Alabama's roads, shackled together by leg irons. In Mississippi, inmates must again wear striped uniforms. The reason for the change is to humiliate the convicts. In other states, inmates are being denied television, tobacco, weight-lifting equipment, and sometimes even visits from family and friends. [10]

Alcatraz, located on an island of rock in San Francisco Bay, held some of the most famous criminals in the United States until it closed in 1963.

TYPES OF PRISONS

The word *prison* conjures up visions of high concrete walls topped with gun towers patrolled by armed guards. For the most part, this is an accurate description of many maximum-security prisons. But prisons, like their inhabitants, fit many descriptions.

One of the most famous prisons in the world is Alcatraz, also known as "the Rock." Situated on 12 acres of solid rock in San Francisco Bay, this island fortress confined some of America's most notorious federal prisoners (such as Al Capone) from 1934 until it closed in 1963. Other American prisons gained notoriety for different reasons. San Quentin's gas chamber (10 miles from San Francisco) and Sing Sing's electric chair (in Ossining, New York) were the sites of many highly publicized executions. And in 1971, the bloodiest prison riot in American history occurred at Attica, an upstate New York correctional facility. Thirty-two inmates and 11 guards were killed when state police stormed Attica to quell the riot.

Inmates of Attica State Prison in New York raised their arms in clenched-fist salutes during the 1971 riot, the bloodiest in American history.

The gas chamber in
San Quentin Prison

Many prisons, however, have no walls or bars. Some arc enclosed by only a fence and others resemble college campuses more than institutions housing convicted criminals.

At the end of 1990, the United States had 1,287 federal and state prisons. Eighty of these were federal prisons, the remainder state prisons. The numbers increase continually as construction on new prisons reaches an all-time high. Since 1980, the prison population has risen 188 percent and will almost certainly continue to increase.[1]

Prisons are known by a variety of names—penitentiaries, reformatories, penal institutions, and correctional facilities. The names reflect the prevailing philosophy toward punishment at the time the prisons were built. Thus, penitentiaries were intended to invoke penitence; reformatories to reform. Most prisons today are simply called *correctional facilities*, apparently because they attempt to correct. Whatever its official name, a prison remains "the joint" to those behind its walls.

Prisons are classified by the amount of freedom allowed within their walls and by their physical structure. Three rather broad classifications are used: maximum security, medium security, and minimum security. Seventy-five percent of all prisons are either medium or minimum security.[2]

As the name implies, maximum-security prisons are characterized by high walls; tiered, rectangular cellblocks lined with individual cells; and mazes of electronically controlled steel gates and barred doors. Among maximum-security prisons, the most secure facility in the country is located in Marion, Illinois. The Marion prison confines the most violent and escape-prone inmates in the federal prison system. Marion is often referred to as "the new Alcatraz." Inmates are confined to individual cells 23 hours a day and never leave their cells unless accompanied by a guard. (By law, all United States prisoners must be given one hour a day to exercise.) At most other maximum-security prisons, inmates spend much of their time outside

When not in their cells, prisoners at the federal prison in Marion, Illinois, are led—one guard to a handcuffed prisoner—to an exercise area.

their cells working, attending school, participating in sports, or socializing in outdoor yards.

In 1995 a new federal prison opened in Florence, Colorado. It will eventually replace the Marion facility as the most secure federal prison. Marion will still be a penitentiary, but it will lose its notoriety as the replacement for Alcatraz.

Medium-security prisons allow more freedom. They are usually enclosed by metal fences that are sometimes lined with coiled razor wire (also known as concertina wire because of its resemblance to the accordianlike musical instrument of that name). Medium-security inmates generally sleep in dormitories or rooms rather than in cells and are less supervised in their activities than prisoners in maximum-security prisons.

The least supervised and most open prisons are the minimum-security institutions, often called honor or trustee camps. Inmates are free to move from one part of the facility to another in minimum-security prisons.

Convicts nearing the end of their sentences in maximum-security prisons sometimes serve the final portion of their terms in minimum-security facilities so they can become accustomed to a less restrictive environment before their release.

Correctional facilities vary considerably in architecture, population, type of inmates, opportunities for schooling and job training, availability of treatment programs, and strictness in enforcement of the rules.

The trend in prison construction today is toward smaller, less restrictive facilities. They are cheaper to build and operate than are the oldtime maximum-security facilities. Most prisons house fewer than 500

This is a typical high- to medium-security unit at the California Department of Corrections.

prisoners. But 26 prisons, 17 of which are located in California, confine more than 2,500 inmates. The largest facility in the country is located in Vacaville, California, and confines nearly 7,500 prisoners.[3]

With their heads shaved, new participants in a "boot camp"
program—an alternative to prison—arrive at their barracks.

3

WHO GOES TO PRISON?

Justice is an abstract concept meaning fairness and impartiality under the law. In some societies, justice is served by cutting off a thief's hand; in others, adulterers are executed. In all societies, however, many people believe that criminals who are rich and influential seem to receive more lenient treatment than others.

How fair is America's criminal justice system? Consider a profile of the typical inmate in an American prison. Most convicts are high school dropouts who grew up poor. Most convicts were unemployed or working in unskilled jobs at the time of their arrest. Most were under the age of 30 when they were first admitted to prison. For the most part, their offenses are included in the F.B.I.'s Index of Crimes: murder, rape, robbery, aggravated assault, burglary, larceny, and motor vehicle theft. These so-called street crimes are committed primarily by men and women we associate with the word *criminal*.

Another category of crime, known as *white-collar crime*, is more lucrative than street crime. White-collar criminals are generally well educated and hold

35

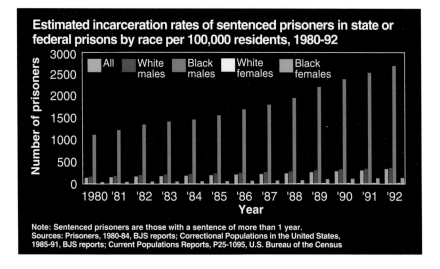

Estimated incarceration rates of sentenced prisoners in state or federal prisons by race per 100,000 residents, 1980-92

Number of prisoners

3000
2500
2000
1500
1000
500
0

All White males Black males White females Black females

1980 '81 '82 '83 '84 '85 '86 '87 '88 '89 '90 '91 '92
Year

Note: Sentenced prisoners are those with a sentence of more than 1 year.
Sources: Prisoners, 1980-84, BJS reports; Correctional Populations in the United States, 1985-91, BJS reports; Current Populations Reports, P25-1095, U.S. Bureau of the Census

high-paying, professional jobs. Doctors, lawyers, bankers, accountants, businesspeople, and government officials are sometimes convicted of white-collar crime. Their crimes are nonviolent offenses such as tax evasion, embezzlement, fraud, political corruption, and stock manipulation. Within the United States, costs of white-collar crime to the public are 10 times greater than the combined total costs from larcenies, robberies, burglaries, and auto thefts.[1] In the words of Superior Court Judge Lance Ito, "More people have suffered from the point of a fountain pen than from the point of a gun."[2]

If white-collar criminals are responsible for such a vast amount of crime, why aren't more of them in prison? Because white-collar criminals do not employ weapons or physically intimidate their victims, the public does not view them with the same fear as they do street criminals. When citizens plead for safer streets, they are not seeking protection from white-collar criminals. While murder, robbery, burglary, and car theft are easy to define, white-collar crimes are not so simple. They are generally paper transactions devised by clever people. In addition to the complexity of their crimes, the ability of white-collar criminals to afford excellent lawyers makes it difficult for prosecutors to obtain convictions.

Prisons have always been populated primarily by street criminals—men and women from the poorest classes of American society. Blacks, in particular, represent a disproportionately high number of prison inmates. Although they comprise only 6 percent of the population of the United States, black males make up 44 percent of the country's prison population. The incarceration rate of black males is more than seven times greater than the rate for white males.[3]

Michael Milken leaves U.S. District Court in New York after pleading innocent to charges of insider trading on the stock exchange, a white-collar crime.

Does the criminal justice system discriminate against blacks? A *Washington Post*-ABC News poll conducted in 1992 found that 89 percent of blacks and 43 percent of whites do not think blacks receive equal treatment in the criminal justice system.[4] A variety of opinions exists about the disproportionate number of blacks in prison. "There is documented evidence that blacks have been treated differently than whites in the criminal justice system,"said Linda Foley, a University of North Florida psychologist.[5]

William Wilbanks, author of a 1987 book, *The Myth of a Racist Criminal Justice System*, disputes that viewpoint, however. "I looked at all the studies produced in English up until about 1985," he states, "and they showed that when you control for other factors, that black and white treatment is equal."[6]

A 1983 study by the Rand Corporation, a nonprofit research organization that studies prisons and sentencing, concluded that neither viewpoint is conclusive. According to Rand researchers, "Studies have offered evidence both for and against racial bias in arrest rates, prosecution, conviction, sentencing, corrections, and parole."[7]

A Bureau of Justice Statistics report claims, "The overrepresentation of blacks among offenders admitted to state prisons occurs because blacks commit a disproportionate number of imprisonable crimes."[8] But Linda Foley says that, "Evidence tends to indicate that juries are sympathetic to people of their own race."[9]

Regardless of race, in recent years a new group of criminals has emerged—people who would not have gone to prison 10 or 15 years ago. This new breed of

Estimated number of adult arrests for selected serious crimes and drug offenses, 1980-92

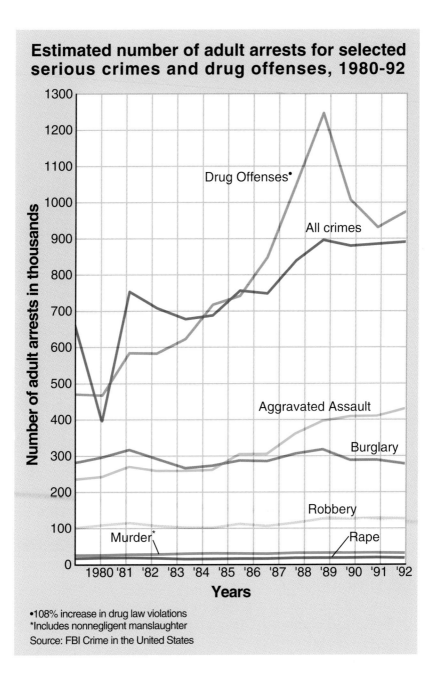

Number of adult arrests in thousands

Drug Offenses*

All crimes

Aggravated Assault

Burglary

Robbery

Murder*

Rape

1980 '81 '82 '83 '84 '85 '86 '87 '88 '89 '90 '91 '92

Years

•108% increase in drug law violations
*Includes nonnegligent manslaughter
Source: FBI Crime in the United States

Half the inmates in the federal prison system are drug
offenders. Many are users, not dealers, of crack cocaine.

inmates resulted from America's "war on drugs"and is
the main cause for the logjam in the courts and the
overflowing jails and prisons.[10]

In an attempt to control the drug problem, the United
States Congress and many state legislatures passed
tougher drug laws—particularly since the appearance
of "crack" cocaine, a potent by-product of pure cocaine. Because crack is more affordable than many
other illegal drugs, more people have become addicted
to it. As a result of stricter laws regarding the use of illegal drugs, more than half the inmates in the federal
prison system are drug offenders. While drug dealing
has always been a serious crime, many of the new offenders are users, not dealers. Within the next few
years, the number of drug offenders in prison is expected to reach 70 percent.[11]

Many new drug laws also call for mandatory prison sentences—sentences that are set and cannot be changed by a judge. In Michigan, for example, a 50-year-old grandmother with no prior criminal record was sentenced to life in prison without parole for possessing more than 650 grams (22 ¾ ounces) of cocaine.[12] Very few murderers receive life sentences without parole.

Because of publicity about jail and prison overcrowding, the public thinks that a massive crime wave is sweeping the country. Much of the increase in prisoners, however, is a result of the stricter drug laws, not the result of a rising crime rate. According to Patrick A. Langan, a Department of Justice statistician, the overall crime rate has actually fallen steadily since 1973.[13] Between 1980 and 1992, however, the number of arrests for drug-law violations increased by 108 percent.[14] In 1960, a mere 4 percent of inmates were sent to prison for drug-related offenses; now, 30 percent of all inmates—federal and state—are behind bars for drug offenses.

Other factors have also contributed to swelling prison populations. Along with generally tougher law-and-order attitudes of prosecutors and judges, many state legislatures have passed laws requiring prison for habitual drunk drivers. Many drug violators and drunk drivers are not "career criminals." They are generally better educated than the traditional convict, are more likely to be employed at the time of their arrest, and are nonviolent. So while the majority of prison inmates are still street criminals, many inmates are imprisoned for crimes that laws did not cover 15 years ago.

Inmates eat from tin plates in the dining room of the maximum-security prison in Buford, Georgia.

INSIDE THE BIG HOUSE

"You don't know what it's like to do time until you've eaten from a tin plate," a Massachusetts convict said. Eating from a tin plate symbolizes the most common sound heard inside a maximum-security prison—the clang of metal. A series of steel-barred gates leads step by step into the core of the prison. Each gate bangs shut before the next one opens. At the heart of every maximum-security prison are cavernous cellblocks—long rectangular units of concrete and steel—lined on each side with individual cells. The average cellblock contains about 300 cells. Some larger prisons contain as many as 10 cellblocks. Here, too, individual cell doors regularly open and close with metallic finality.

In the mess hall, prisoners slide stainless steel trays along tubular stainless steel counters. Fellow prisoners plop food onto each tray with metal spoons. Even in the still of the night, the bang of an opening or closing cell door will occasionally echo, like distant thunder, as guards respond to a medical emergency, a suicide, or to remove someone who has "flipped out."

New inmates spend several days isolated from the general population while they are processed—photographed, assigned a number, issued prison clothing, examined physically and given psychological, aptitude, and intelligence tests. Prison staff members evaluate rap sheets (police records) for violent tendencies or attitude problems and note special skills or expertise in a particular occupation. Following this evaluation, each newcomer is assigned a job and permanent living quarters—a nine-by-six-foot cell equipped with a cot, toilet bowl, sink, and small metal desk attached to the wall. The prisoner is now in the *mainline*, the general prison population.

Certain jobs exist in all prisons. Floors must be mopped, clothing and bedding laundered, food prepared and served, electrical and plumbing repairs made. These jobs are assigned to inmates. There are classrooms, a barbershop, a tailor shop for mending and altering clothes, and most likely a print shop. Various offices employ a handful of inmate clerks. Beyond these unskilled or semiskilled jobs, however, most prisons offer little in the way of job training that can be used on the outside. About one in four prison inmates is idle, neither assigned to a job nor enrolled in a school program.[1]

A United States Bureau of Prisons study of 7000 federal prisoners showed that those who were trained for jobs behind bars were more likely to hold jobs when released and less likely to slide back into crime. Only six percent of those inmates who were trained in useful occupations while in prison, the study revealed, violated their parole or were arrested within a year of their release—far lower than the repeat-crime rate for other inmates. Bureau of Prisons chief Michael Quinlan says, "Prison industries can break the cycle of crime."[2]

Despite the evidence that job training lowers the recidivism (repeat offender) rate, fewer than one in ten inmates in the United States has a job that might lead to employment after release. In dollars and cents alone, it would seem to make sense for prisons to provide useful job training programs. The cost of keeping an inmate in prison runs between $12,000 and $24,000 a year.

"For that kind of money you can send a kid to Harvard," says writer Richard Greene. And in some places, such as New York, the cost of housing an inmate can run as high as $30,000 a year. To which Greene adds, "Now we're talking about sending a kid for summer study and travel in Europe as well."[3]

With so many experts in agreement on the value of job training, why do so few opportunities exist for prisoners to prepare themselves to be self-supporting upon their release?

Not everyone supports the idea of training and educating prisoners. Many law-abiding citizens who cannot afford college or vocational school for themselves resent having their hard-earned tax dollars spent to educate convicted criminals. Labor unions and private businesses also raise objections. With so many people unemployed in the United States, labor unions argue, is it fair that criminals trained in prison at taxpayers' expense should come out and take jobs away from honest job seekers? Private businesses question how they can compete with prison-run industries, where labor costs are a fraction of the minimum wage.

Because of overcrowding, two prisoners often share one cell.

Despite this opposition, however, some state and federal prisons offer educational and job-training opportunities. The most extensive program is a little-known government corporation called Federal Prison Industries (FPI). By law, FPI can do business only with the government. It manufactures everything from electrical cables for the army to Smoky Bear signs for the nation's parks. About 14,000 federal inmates are involved in FPI.[4]

Private firms have also set up 74 work programs in various states, in which convicts earn the minimum wage or more. For example, inmates make baseball caps in Connecticut and leather goods in Alaska. In Nevada they are repairing a casino's historic auto collection.[5]

At the Correctional Institution for Women in North

Carolina, 10 inmate volunteers handle nearly 23,000 calls a month to the state's toll-free number for tourist information. Down the hall from the telephone room, five other female inmates stuff and label some of the 250,000 packets of tourist information that the state mails out each year. While the desire to rehabilitate inmates inspired the program, budgetary considerations also played a part. Thomas Harper, a supervisor in North Carolina's Travel and Tourism Division, estimates that the state saves $150,000 a year in salaries and benefits by using prison inmates.[6]

Convicts staff their own radio station in Dade County, Florida. Here, they are taking a break from the "Inmate Evening News."

Cornelia Gonzalez, who is serving 22 years for drug trafficking, is enthusiastic about the program. "I love this job," she says. "When I get out of here, I'm going to settle down and get a job in tourism."[7] About a dozen other states from Oregon to Maryland have also turned to inmates to assist with travel and tourism inquiries.

Most states employ a limited number of inmates in prison trades, primarily in the manufacture of products used in state facilities. Some people question how well prison job skills translate into job skills on the outside. Modern technology and job markets change so quickly that cumbersome prison bureaucracies are rarely able to keep pace, which makes many of the skills learned in prison obsolete by the time an inmate is released.

Nearly every prison in America offers high school courses leading to General Equivalency Diplomas (GEDs). Many also offer accredited college courses. For the large number of men and women who can't read or write when they enter prison, academic learning can be a tremendous boost to their self-confidence and improve their suitability for outside employment.

Sometimes profound personality changes occur after exposure to education. Otis Tate, an inmate at Oak Park Heights Prison in Minnesota, did not learn to read or write until he was in his early twenties. Fifty-one-year-old Tate has spent most of his adult life in some of the nation's harshest prisons. Born into an impoverished family of 10 children, he learned the art of survival early in life. His sister Barbara recalls a scene from their childhood: "We didn't have any food. Our mother felt bad, but there wasn't anything she could do. Otis went around the corner, broke into a store, and took some food. That's when it started," she says, referring to her brother's criminal career.[8]

At Oak Park Heights, Tate completed an associate of arts degree with a B+ average, carrying a stiff load of 21 to 24 college credits each quarter. His next goal is to earn a bachelor's degree. And when he is a free man again? He would like to work with Habitat for Humanity, or the Cooperative for American Relief to Everywhere (CARE), or the Peace Corps. "I want to get involved," he says. In response to his long criminal record, he simply replies, "I'm not like that anymore."[9]

Donald V. Stanley, 27, is another example of a success story involving education and job training in prison. Stanley spent four years in a California prison where he earned a junior college degree. He also worked as a reservations agent in a Trans World Airlines booking center set up inside the prison. Following his parole 18 months ago, Stanley was hired by TWA as a full-time reservations agent.

Newly promoted, he proudly states, "I'm living proof that it's worth giving people a second chance."[10]

Although this scene is from a movie (Blood In, Blood Out: Bound by Honor), *violence among prison inmates is common.*

PRISON VIOLENCE

Males between the ages of 15 and 24 commit the majority of crimes in the United States. Ninety-four percent of all inmates in correctional facilities, both juvenile and adult, are male.[1] Referring to murder rates for young males, James Fox, dean of Northeastern University's College of Criminal Justice, says, "In examining homicide rates, there is the bad news, then there is the really bad news. Murder rates among 18- to 24-year-olds are up 65 percent since 1985, and murder rates among 14- to 17-year-olds are up 165 percent."[2] The murder rate among white male teenagers has doubled in the past decade, and the rate for black male teens has tripled. "Not only are teenagers becoming more ruthless, they are also increasing in numbers," Fox adds.[3]

Experts offer several reasons for this upsurge of violence: the easy availability of guns, particularly lethal weapons like .357 magnums, 9mm semiautomatics, and UZI assault rifles; more violence in movies and television; the growth of gangs and drug trafficking; lack of discipline in homes and schools; and poverty in urban ghettos.

Not surprisingly, violence is reflected in America's prisons, where society's most violent offenders usually end up. Deep scars slash Otis Tate's torso—vivid reminders of several prison stabbings. "The law of the jungle is," he says, "if you're going to survive you have to move and move fast."[4]

In the old days, prisoners feared brutal guards. Now the fear permeating American prisons comes mostly from fellow convicts. Beatings, stabbings, and homosexual rapes are everyday occurrences. Because of the threat from other inmates, more and more prisoners are requesting protective custody, even though that means being locked up for 23 hours a day.

Overcrowding is a major factor in prison violence. Double-bunking, dormitories filled beyond capacity, and gymnasiums and recreation rooms converted into makeshift sleeping quarters all contribute to increased tension in prisons. Bulging prison populations also place more pressure on correctional officers. Because supervision is spread thin, aggressive inmates can more easily prey on weaker ones. According to *Corrections Compendium*, a journal for corrections professionals, 47 homicides occurred in U.S. prisons in 1993; 1 staff member was murdered; 4,829 staff members were assaulted; 8,295 inmates were assaulted by other inmates; and 100 suicides occurred.[5]

Psychological violence—the *threat* of violence that weaker inmates suffer—is more difficult to measure. To keep from being beaten, weaker prisoners are regularly coerced into giving sexual favors and personal items, such as candy, cigarettes, clothing, and food. Reverend Manning Moore, a chaplain at Lorton Prison in Virginia, told of one inmate's concern for his personal safety: "A young man came to my office for a counseling session; his wife was present, too. He hadn't been raped, but there had been threats, and he was so terrified that he broke down and wept."[6]

When former heavyweight boxing champion Mike Tyson was sentenced to six years in prison in 1992, there was concern about his safety in the Indiana prison system. Zachary Taylor, an inmate, commented: "There are guys who'll run extortion on [try to take

Heavyweight boxing champion Mike Tyson was sentenced to six years in prison in 1992. He was granted parole in March 1995.

Because of overcrowded prisons, staff members are forced to find makeshift sleeping quarters for inmates.

money from] him. Tyson may be vicious, but we have guys in here who are barbaric . . . . A left jab ain't going to get it. It would be flesh against steel."[7]

Other than a couple of minor disciplinary problems, Tyson survived his three years in prison without incident. He was paroled from the Indiana Youth Center on March 25, 1995, expecting to resume his professional boxing career.

The head of Indiana's Civil Liberties Union, Richard Waples, states bluntly: "Indiana's prison system stinks."[8] According to Scripps Howard News Service, "Indiana's prisons have been marked by violence and seethe with racial unrest. Inmate gangs control drug traffic, homosexual prostitution, protection rackets, and contract murders. Gangs use rapes, beatings, stabbings, and sometimes death to enforce inmate law in a system

that incarcerates 14,500 criminals—nearly twice as many as Colorado, a state of similar size."[9]

The problem, apparently, is not only with inmates. "We're finding 40 to 60 percent of the officers in the Indiana system are failing drug tests," says an internal prison investigator. "Nothing is being done about that."[10]

Another factor contributing to prison violence is racial tension. A New York convict wrote of frequent conflicts between black and Hispanic inmates at his facility. "It doesn't take much to start these two factions fighting," he said. And on the West Coast, especially in California, prison gangs are formed along racial lines. Major gangs include the white Aryan Brotherhood, the Mexican Mafia, and the Black Guerrilla Family. Reverend Jude Siciliano, a Dominican priest for six years at San Quentin, said the potential for violence is so great that the recreation yards have been segregated according to gang affiliation. "It's really warfare at San Quentin," he observed.[11]

Even consensual homosexual (gay) relationships often lead to conflict. "An inmate becomes possessive of a [gay prisoner] as if it was his wife," a New York convict reports. "He'll fight anyone who insults or teases him."[12]

This same inmate remarked that drug transactions were the most common cause of assaults at his facility.[13] How do inmates acquire weapons and drugs in prison? Drugs are smuggled in by relatives, friends, or guards. Most weapons are crudely fashioned from virtually any piece of metal or rigid plastic. Kitchen knives and forks, screwdrivers and other metal tools, steel rods from bedsprings—even toothbrushes—can be sharpened into lethal pointed weapons. Dumbbells used in weight lifting provide another common weapon. They are often employed in "pipings"—10 pounds of solid steel striking against the skull.

Councilman Peter Vallone described the New York City prison on Riker's Island as "the largest penal colony in the world."[14] Situated in the East River and accessible only by bridge, Riker's consists of nine buildings housing 14,000 inmates. On August 7, 1990, Rikers lived up to its reputation as one of the most violent prisons in the country when a guard was mugged inside the prison. Correctional officer Steven Narby was cornered by three inmates at a stairwell. They broke his jaw and a rib and robbed him of his jewelry, including a gold chain.[15]

Not all prisons are hotbeds of violence, of course. Because bad news generally tends to dominate the headlines, prisons do not receive much attention until a problem arises—a riot or a scandal. A little known program to combat violence, the Alternatives to Violence Project (AVP), has been developing in the New York prison system for nearly 20 years. AVP was inspired by a group of "lifers" (inmates serving lifetime sentences) in 1975. Inmate trainers—men who have successfully completed both basic and advanced workshops—operate the program. AVP examines the causes of violence, how violence increases, and how to calm potentially violent confrontations.

"I grew up in a violent neighborhood," says Lowell Thomas, an inmate serving 20 years to life. "It [violence] was how you solved all conflict. Through AVP, my attitude has changed dramatically."[16]

Says Vince Mojica, an AVP trainer serving 15 years to life: "It's the only program that is really working to provide rehabilitation for inmates."[17]

Another AVP trainer, George Lombardo, sums up his outlook: "Jails tend to build hatred. AVP is the only program aimed at reducing violence that works. This program will get people out and help them to stay there."[18]

Female inmates at the Central California Women's Facility pick up litter.

WOMEN IN PRISON

Although women comprise only about six percent of the state and federal prison population in the United States, their numbers have been increasing at a faster rate than that of men. The female prison population increased by almost 10 percent from 1992 to 1993, while the male prison population rose by slightly more than 7 percent. At the end of 1993, a record 55,365 women were incarcerated in state and federal prisons.[1] In 1980 the female prison population was 12,331; in 1985, 21,296; in 1990, 40,484.[2]

Why this steep rise? For the most part, the reasons are the same as those offered to explain crime in general: the breakup of families, poverty, increased drug use, affiliation with gangs, lack of jobs. Drugs, however, appear to be the biggest influence on the increase in crime among women. Female inmates are more likely than males to have used a major illegal drug (heroin, cocaine, crack, LSD, or PCP) in the month before their current offense. More than twice as many women as men report using a major illegal drug daily.

Among convicted female inmates:

—Almost half say they committed their offenses while under the influence of drugs or alcohol.

—About 54 percent had used drugs in the month before their current offense.

—Nearly 24 percent say they committed their current crime for money to buy drugs.[3]

The characteristics of female prisoners are similar to those of males—with the exception of marital status and pre-arrest employment. A higher percentage of women are married at the time of their arrest, and women are less likely than men to be working the month before their arrest.

Three-fourths of women in prison were convicted of homicide, fraud, larceny, robbery, or a drug offense. Half the female inmates are between the ages of 25 and 34. The ethnic breakdown among females is nearly identical to that of males: 46 percent black, 36 percent white, 14 percent Hispanic, and 4 percent "other" (Native Americans, Alaskan Eskimos, Asians, and Pacific Islanders).[4]

Most women's prisons are a combination of maximum, medium, and minimum security. Very few resemble the walled facilities confining men. Generally, *holding rooms* exist at each facility for violent inmates and those requiring disciplinary lockdowns.

The Minnesota Correctional Facility in Shakopee, Minnesota, has a large lawn that surrounds the unfenced cluster of brick buildings that confine about 200 prisoners. Impeccably landscaped, the grounds at Shakopee reflect the efforts—and obvious pride—of the prison's horticulture program.

Members of the staff are called correctional officers. According to Parenting/Family Director Michele Kopfman, "Their primary responsibility is supervision, but they are trained counselors as well." In addition to the administration building, five separate buildings— or units—house the inmates at Shakopee. Two units have 32 rooms, and three others have 45 rooms. At the center of each unit is a control desk staffed by a correctional counselor. Behind the desk are electronically controlled switches for locking and opening rooms and an intercom system that is connected to each room.

Former correctional officer Tami Prestin explained the operation in the Tubman Unit: "Unless there's a disturbance, the rooms are never locked," Prestin says. "For the safety of the other inmates we'll occasionally lock down the entire unit. For instance, a while back we had a woman threatening someone with a glass coffee pot. In a situation like that, we order everyone to their rooms and lock them in until the disturbance is under control. But we don't get the amount of violence you hear about in men's prisons. Mostly it's a lot of screaming and yelling."

Correctional officers maintain discipline by giving extra privileges for good behavior and initiative. The officers evaluate each new inmate during Receiving and Orientation (R & O). Together, the officer and the inmate establish various educational and personal development goals. Each woman targets a series of attainment levels. As an inmate reaches each level, she is awarded additional privileges, such as extended visits, off-grounds educational opportunities, volunteer community projects, or furloughs (authorized leaves of absence).

Women in federal and state prisons, 1991

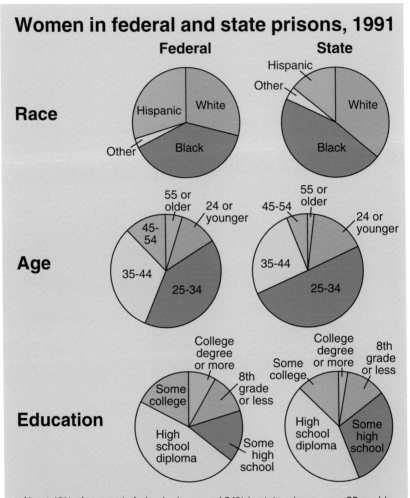

•About 48% of women in federal prisons and 34% in state prisons were 35 or older.
•An estimated 29% of women in federal prisons compared to 17% in state prisons
 were married.
•Almost 26% of women in federal prisons and 16% in state facilities had some
 education at the college level.
•About 20% of women in federal prisons and 2% in state prisons were noncitizens.
•Just over 63% of women in federal prisons, compared to 47% in state prisons,
 were employed before their offense. A quarter of women in federal prisons and a
 third in state prisons were unemployed and not looking for work.

Source: U.S. Department of Justice, Bureau of Justice Statistics

The ultimate reward for self-initiative at Shakopee is the Independent Living Center—a unit consisting of six apartments—each of which has two bedrooms, a kitchenette, a living area, and a bathroom. This center is reserved for women who have earned the highest level of trust during their imprisonment. Minimal staff supervision and many off-grounds programs accompany this privileged status.

Inmates can enter a number of programs, including chemical dependency programs, education and industry workshops, parenting and family counseling programs, and sessions on many phases of personal development. In addition to the wide range of self-improvement opportunities, an equally extensive recreation program exists. A gymnasium with an exercise-fitness area, an outdoor volleyball court, and a softball field are available to inmates. Additional activities at Shakopee include aerobics, ceramics, plays, and card tournaments.

Few people dispute the need for chemical dependency counseling and seminars on parenting and personal improvement for prisoners, but perceived luxuries like bowling alleys and tennis courts raise eyebrows. Some people grumble about the country club atmosphere and bristle at the extravagant niceties provided to convicted criminals at taxpayers' expense.

Others contend that since most prison inmates never enjoyed the privileges taken for granted by middle-class Americans, these perks will help prisoners become better human beings. For men and women raised in poverty and broken families, some argue, a few "luxuries" will have a positive effect.

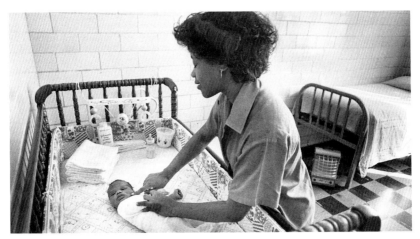

Mother and baby share a room at the Florida Correctional Institution for Women. The wisdom of raising children in prisons is a debatable issue.

More than three-quarters of all women in prison have children. An estimated 25,700 female inmates in 1993 had more than 56,000 children under the age of 18. Who cares for those children in their mothers' absence?

Among women in prison who had young children:

—A quarter said that at least one child was living with the father.

—Half said their children were with a grandparent.

—A fifth of the children were with other relatives.

—Less than a tenth said their children were in a foster home or other institution.[5]

A parent's imprisonment, however, creates problems that go beyond the disruption of each family. According to figures compiled by the U.S. Justice Department, more than half of all juveniles imprisoned in state institutions have immediate family members who have also been incarcerated. The same is true for more than a third of adult criminals in local jails and state prisons. Some criminologists say that these statistics provide striking evidence for the theory that criminality tends to run in families.[6]

Previous abuse may also be a factor in determining who commits crimes. An estimated 44 percent of women in prison reported that they had been either physically or sexually abused at some time in their lives. Thirty-two percent said this abuse occurred before age 18. Compared to men, women were three times more likely to have been abused before age 18 and five times more likely to have been abused at age 18 or after.[7] The expression "violence begets violence" seems apparent in the statistics. Women and men serving time for violent crimes were much more likely to have been abused than were nonviolent offenders.[8]

A distinctive criminal pattern is also apparent in female drug abusers. Addiction routinely leads to prostitution and drug dealing. In a play called *Living a Hard Life*, written and performed by inmates at the Volunteers of America Regional Corrections Center for Women in Roseville, Minnesota, actors vividly portrayed a glimpse of street life. The play explores the downward spiral of drug dealing, addiction, and prostitution.

One of the female performers, a 29-year-old named Sugar, commented after the play: "That's exactly how it is. It's a very sad way to live."[9]

Lynette, the 20-year-old author of the gritty drama, explains her intended message: "It's trying to say there's a better way of living than being into prostitution and drugs."[10]

Teenage boys stand waiting in the hall of a juvenile detention facility.

JUVENILE
LOCKUPS

I'm in camp for attempted robbery. Two of my home-boys ran one way and me and my homie ran another way, but not faster than the German shepherd dogs that caught us. When I finally do all my sentence at camp, I hope someday I will be somebody special. Go-ing to school and getting good grades was always hard for me. But, buddy, you ain't never seen nothin' harder than doin' time in jail.

My name that all my friends and enemies know me by is my street name LT. I am at the age of 15 turning 16 in 2 months. I've been a gangbanger for 3 years and in and out of jail since the age of 14. It came to the point where I loved my homies more than my own fam-ily. I'm back in juvenile hall again. It's sad to have a to-tal stranger run your life and have all your freedom taken away right under your nose. I lost many friends cause of gangs and it ain't fun any more!!!

I started causing trouble as soon as I entered junior high school . . . . Ditching, burglarizing homes, stealing cars, and drinking just to impress the homeboyz and prove I wasn't a punk.[1]

These letters were excerpted from a book entitled *Letters to You from Teenagers in Jail.* All the letter writers were gangbangers (gang members) locked up in Los Angeles juvenile jails. About 93,000 juveniles are confined in correctional facilities in the United States.[2] A very small percentage belong to gangs, but whether big-city gangbangers or small-town delinquents, a thread of similarity runs through their backgrounds.

A high percentage come from broken homes and poor families. The majority were below-average students or had dropped out of school altogether. Most, 94 percent, are in custody for delinquency offenses (serious crimes); 5 percent for status offenses (truancy, running away from home, incorrigibility, underage drinking); and approximately 1 percent because they were abused, neglected, or dependent youngsters who had nowhere else to go. Over half are in custody because of drug- or alcohol-related offenses.[3]

In most states, anyone under 18 is considered a juvenile. Occasionally, when a juvenile commits a very serious crime—murder, for example—he or she is tried in adult court. Violent habitual offenders are also tried as adults. "It's a horrendous problem," says Hennepin County District Judge Beryl Nord, a former Minnesota juvenile court judge. He remembers trying to find a treatment alternative for a 12-year-old homicide suspect. "Once you send them up to St. Cloud (a maximum-security prison), you've given up on them. You've thrown them away."[4]

However, former Minnesota Corrections Commissioner Orville Pung believes behavior, not age, should determine where to send criminals. "Some of these kids are more predatory than the older inmates, and that's what got them certified [tried as adults]."[5]

Prisons—at least in name—do not exist in the juvenile correctional system, even though some juvenile institutions are every bit as secure as many adult prisons. Like adults, juveniles are assigned to institutions according to their prior records and the severity of their crimes. While the most hardened adults are sent to penitentiaries, the oldest and toughest juveniles are sent to state training schools—the juvenile equivalent to a penitentiary. Although younger adult criminals are sent to reformatories, the youngest and least serious juvenile offenders are confined in county homes. Less severe facilities include forestry camps and honor farms for adults. Foster-care homes for status offenders and children removed from their homes because of parental neglect are the least severe juvenile facilities, but they are often not available.

The issues raised concerning juvenile facilities are the same as those of adult prisons. Namely, are correctional settings capable of rehabilitating anyone? Many professionals in the field of juvenile delinquency contend that correctional facilities are merely "schools for crime." A surprising number of delinquents, according to one study, apparently feel that prison in general should be tougher. Arnold Goldstein, director of the Center for Research on Aggression at Syracuse

University, surveyed 250 juvenile delinquents about their solutions to violence. Most agreed that jail was too "cushy."[6]

Almost everyone involved with the juvenile justice system agrees that too many children of negligent parents end up in reform schools. Even though they have not broken any laws, they are thrown in with hard-core delinquents because of a legal concept known as *parens patriae.* Literally translated, this term means "parent as king." When parents are deemed unfit because of neglect or abuse, the government becomes the legal parent. Many of these children are placed in county homes with delinquents when foster care is not available.

Another group of youngsters who often end up in correctional settings are status offenders, those who have broken laws that apply only to juveniles. Truancy

Truancy—staying away from school without permission—is a status offense handled in juvenile court.

Dinnertime at a juvenile detention facility

(staying out of school without permission), running away from home, underage drinking, and incorrigibility (repeated refusal to behave or reform) are status offenses. While abused and neglected children are processed through family courts, status offenders are handled in juvenile courts along with delinquents.

Juvenile court judges try to keep these offenders out of jail whenever possible, but chronic status offenders and children from unfit homes often end up in reform schools simply because no other place is available. The argument that rehabilitation is impossible in a correctional environment—that associating with criminal types creates a negative influence—seems particularly true with children whose only "crime" may have been skipping school or having bad parents.

Juveniles accused of a crime are detained in a juvenile detention center (JC or juvie hall) until released into the custody of a parent or guardian or until the case is decided in court. Depending on the circumstances, this process may take anywhere from several hours to several months. As a rule, juvenile detention centers are maximum-security units—as escape-proof as most adult jails.

Juvenile court judges have considerable leeway in choosing what type of facility best fits each individual. There are long-term and short-term facilities, open environments, and institutional environments. More than half of the juveniles confined in correctional facilities in the United States are in long-term institutional environments—that is, state-run training schools. Over 90 percent of long-term institutional inmates are there for delinquent offenses, and the average age ranges from 14 to 17. As in adult prisons, about 95 percent of juveniles in custody are males.

In both adult and juvenile corrections, the trend in recent years has been toward smaller, community-based facilities for nonviolent offenders. Many experts favor eliminating large institutions completely, but some juvenile training schools still confine as many as several hundred children.

A move toward community-based facilities occurred in Massachusetts when Jerome G. Miller headed the Department of Youth Services. "I closed down every reform school in the state," he says. "I was told there'd be an explosion of crime. In fact, the opposite happened."[7]

And how, exactly, did he accomplish this remarkable feat? "We took the money we were spending on

Juvenile detention centers are usually maximum-security facilities.

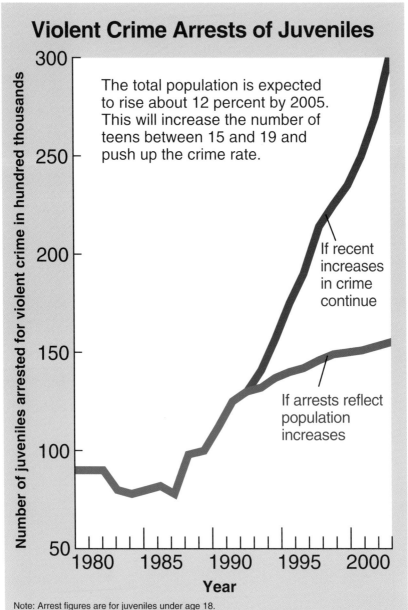

Violent Crime Arrests of Juveniles

The total population is expected to rise about 12 percent by 2005. This will increase the number of teens between 15 and 19 and push up the crime rate.

If recent increases in crime continue

If arrests reflect population increases

Number of juveniles arrested for violent crime in hundred thousands

300
250
200
150
100
50

1980   1985   1990   1995   2000

Year

Note: Arrest figures are for juveniles under age 18.
Source: Basic data: FBI's Crime Reports 1980-1992, National Council on Crime and Delinquency

reform schools and used it to buy a wide variety of services, kid by kid. Every case is different, and we treated each one individually, always aiming not to punish but to divert."[8]

A distinctly pessimistic viewpoint, on the other hand, is offered by Judge David B. Mitchell, an associate judge of the Baltimore City Circuit Court: "Most juvenile institutions are simply little prisons where inmates make contacts for future criminal activities. Innovation in community services and treatment is no longer being fostered . . . . No one wants to pay for it."[9]

These opposite points of view illustrate the wide differences of opinion about juvenile correctional facilities from state to state. Everyone seems to agree on one point, however: even though juvenile facilities don't have walls or bars, they don't appear to be any more effective at rehabilitation than adult prisons.

The grim results of a Minnesota study on youth recidivism even surprised pessimists in the field. In order to track short- and long-term results, the report studied offenders from 1985 and 1991. Some of its more startling findings include:

•Between 53 and 77 percent of male offenders sent to a residential corrections facility (reform school) in 1991 were arrested again within two years.

•More than 90 percent of juvenile offenders released from the state's most restrictive facilities in 1985 had adult records before they turned 23. Nearly 70 percent went to prison.

•Of the juveniles tried as adults and sent to state prison, 84 percent returned within five years of their release.[10]

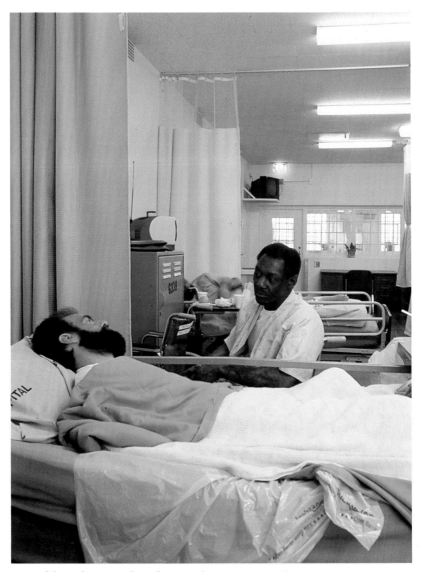

Although a test that detects the presence of HIV in a person's blood is easily available, the question of mass testing prison inmates is controversial. HIV-positive inmates at the California Medical Facility's new HIV Center receive comprehensive care and treatment.

AIDS—A CORRECTIONAL TIME BOMB

Since AIDS (acquired immunodeficiency syndrome) was first identified in 1981, more than 360,000 cases have been reported in the United States as of December 1993. More than 221,000 of these victims have died.[1] AIDS remains one of the country's most difficult and complex public health issues. As of this writing, there is no cure for AIDS, which causes severe damage to the body's immune system—the system that fights off illnesses. When the immune system breaks down, a person can develop life-threatening illnesses.

The time between acquiring the initial HIV infection and the actual onset of AIDS varies considerably among individuals (up to 10 years), but virtually everyone infected with HIV will eventually develop AIDS. At least 80 percent of persons diagnosed as having HIV before 1987 have died.[2]

The virus is transmitted in three ways: through the exchange of blood, semen, and vaginal secretions. The activities that are most likely to transmit HIV are sex and the sharing of hypodermic needles during drug use.

77

Originally, homosexual and bisexual men were the largest groups affected by AIDS, followed by drug users. But in recent years, needle-sharing drug users have become the largest group. One-third of AIDS cases in the United States now originates from drug use. Among female prison inmates, 10 percent of those who had shared needles while taking drugs tested positive for HIV.[3] Because of the large number of former intravenous drug users and the prevalence of homosexual activity in prisons, inmates are at a particularly high risk of contracting AIDS while serving their sentences. At the end of 1991, a total of 17,479 federal and state prison inmates in the United States had been infected with HIV (human immunodeficiency virus), the virus that causes AIDS. That means 2.2 percent of the entire prison population were infected with HIV at that time. In 1991, 528 prison inmates died from AIDS—28 percent of the total number of prison deaths for that year.[4]

Prison administrators are faced with a number of thorny issues as AIDS cases continue to increase in correctional facilities. For example, should HIV testing be mandatory for all inmates? Should infected prisoners be segregated? And if so, to what extent? What is the best way to educate inmates about the disease, and what type of training should be made available to prison staff? Should the confidentiality of HIV-infected patients be protected? How can administrators relieve fears among staff and inmates concerning casual contact with infected prisoners? Should condoms, which can prevent the spread of the disease during sexual intercourse, be made available to inmates? What precautionary measures should be taken to protect inmates

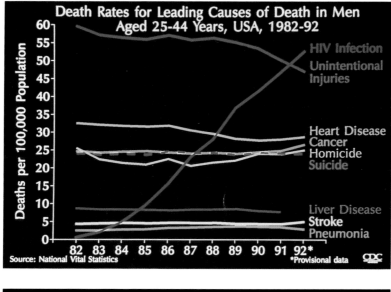

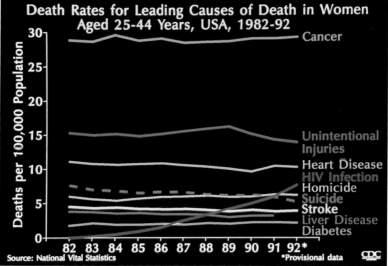

AIDS is on the rise as a major cause of death among both men and women in the United States.

and staff? Should those who test positive for HIV, even though they have no symptoms, be treated the same as those who have AIDS?

Considerable controversy surrounds each of these questions. Strained prison budgets, protection of one group at the expense of others, and the amount and type of available treatment raise additional issues.

Policies differ from state to state, county to county, city to city, and prison to prison. Many of these policies have been challenged by inmates and correctional staff—in city and county jails as well as prisons—and have led to changes in how AIDS-related issues are handled in all correctional settings.

Two major AIDS-related lawsuits were concluded in 1990. In *Harris v. Thigpen*, Alabama inmates challenged the state's policies of mass testing for HIV and

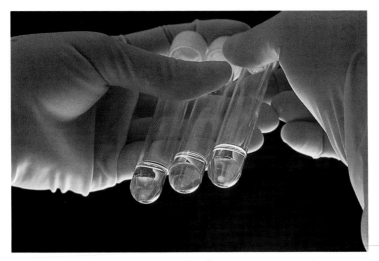

The drug AZT has prolonged the lives of some AIDS patients, but it is expensive. Policies about treatment for prisoners vary from state to state.

segregation of HIV-infected inmates. In January 1990, the court ruled in favor of the correctional department. In a similar challenge to segregation in a California lawsuit—*Gates v. Deukmejian*—a settlement was negotiated in which HIV-infected inmates would live in a closed, but not separate, unit. Also, they would be allowed to participate with other prisoners in all programs and activities.[5]

Medical treatment for AIDS patients is very expensive. For budgetary reasons, some correctional departments treat AIDS patients but not HIV-infected persons. Even though drugs such as AZT (azidothymidine) have proved effective in delaying the onset of AIDS in some HIV patients, treatment is often too costly to provide to patients before they have AIDS.

Many state laws protect the privacy and anonymity of those tested for HIV. From the number of lawsuits initiated by inmates, however, it is obvious that breaches of confidentiality are common. Correctional officers are understandably concerned about who they are dealing with in an environment in which the potential for violence—thus, exposure to blood—is frequent.

AIDS is a relatively recent disease, and research is continually being updated as new facts are discovered. As more information becomes known about the disease, correctional policies also change. At present, methods of dealing with AIDS in correctional facilities are still evolving and adapting to court decisions as well as the latest medical findings.

There are no gun towers or security fences at conservation camps like this one in California. Inmates, however, must stay within marked boundaries.

ALTERNATIVES TO PRISON

The search for solutions to prison overcrowding prodded Americans to examine other ways of dealing with criminals. In the process, several long-held beliefs were challenged. For example, few people still believe that prisons transform criminals into good citizens. Most experts also concede that the majority of men and women now in prison are nonviolent. They are not escape risks and therefore don't require walls and bars. Perhaps the most compelling reason for seeking other ways of handling criminals, though, is the high cost of building enough prisons to house America's expanding correctional population.

Building prisons and jails is big business these days. Tough new laws and mandatory sentences have pushed prisons and jails beyond their capacities. Court orders to relieve overcrowding have placed additional pressure on already strained state budgets. In response, states have spent over $30 billion on prison and jail construction in the past 10 years.[1]

Modern prison design reflects new and changing

philosophies as well as cost consciousness. Most newer prisons bear little resemblance to traditional penitentiaries. Modules and pods (small self-contained units) are now the trend in prison architecture. Several units can be housed in one central building, each unit operating independently of the others. This design helps avoid the potential dangers involved when large numbers of prisoners congregate in one place. Instead of several hundred inmates crowding into a mess hall at one time, meals are prepared in a common kitchen and delivered separately to each unit.

Guards agree that such an arrangement is safer for them as well as for inmates. Most riots occur when large numbers of inmates take over a cellblock or when a fight begins in a recreation yard or dining hall with the entire prison population present.

Some states are also experimenting with privately owned or privately managed prisons. Prison management companies have multiplied as costs increase. Privately operated, profit-oriented prisons, however, could radically lower standards as costs are trimmed. Although private firms claim savings of five to ten percent over government-operated facilities, some experts believe these savings are achieved by reversing many of the reforms acquired through the years.

In an effort to create jobs, the economically depressed town of Appleton, Minnesota, built a $28 million, 494-bed facility before it even had any prisoners. The town expects to profit from the national enthusiasm for locking up lawbreakers. With so many prisons facing court orders to ease prison overcrowding, Appleton's civic leaders saw prisons as a growing industry.

Others view building more prisons as wasteful as well as counterproductive. Modern prisons may be more efficient, but they won't stem the tide of crime, claim critics of the rush to build more prisons. "Prison works to reduce crime only if you don't let the inmates out— ever," says Jerry Miller, a former corrections official.[2]

While prison construction is booming, some states are experimenting with other alternatives to imprisonment for nonviolent property offenders (such as drunk drivers), white collar criminals, forgers, burglars, car thieves, and minor drug offenders.

One of the least costly and most innovative alternatives is electronic home monitoring (EHM). This system allows a convicted person to remain at home or at work while an electronic bracelet attached to the ankle "stands guard." The bracelets are programmed into a computer in the telephone. If a prisoner roams too far from the phone (usually around 150 feet), the computer senses the motion and automatically calls the police. Electronic monitoring allows prisoners to work at their regular jobs rather than being incarcerated at an average annual cost of $20,000. Monitors can distinguish between trips to work and attempts to escape, thus enabling prisoners to earn income to pay for their bracelets, support their families, and pay court costs and restitution. The bracelets can even be programmed to detect the use of alcohol or drugs.[3]

In Philadelphia, the state parole board uses bracelets to keep tabs on parolees. A computer memorizes the sound of the parolee's voice saying the names of 22 different states. It phones the parolee at random hours to request a new combination of eight of those

Electronic home monitoring (EHM) is an effective and economical alternative to prison. An electronic ankle "bracelet" monitors the convicted person's whereabouts. It can even detect the use of drugs and alcohol.

states. If the wrong voice answers, the computer calls the parole board.[4]

How reliable are these devices? "When I first tried them I was skeptical," said Richard Brazil, assistant chief probation officer in California's Humboldt County. "But they've been very successful. Only two people have cut their bracelets off," said Brazil. "But we caught them—we always catch them."[5]

The idea for electronic home-monitoring originated with a comic strip. In 1979 a New Mexico judge noticed that Kingpin—underworld archenemy of Spiderman—was able to effectively monitor the superhero with the aid of an electronic bracelet. The judge asked several computer companies to design something similar. In 1985 a former Honeywell executive came up with a workable device that quickly grew into a successful industry.[6]

First-time offenders and nonviolent criminals are sometimes given an alternative to prison. They might be sentenced to do community service projects, such as cleaning up parks and highways. Intensive supervision

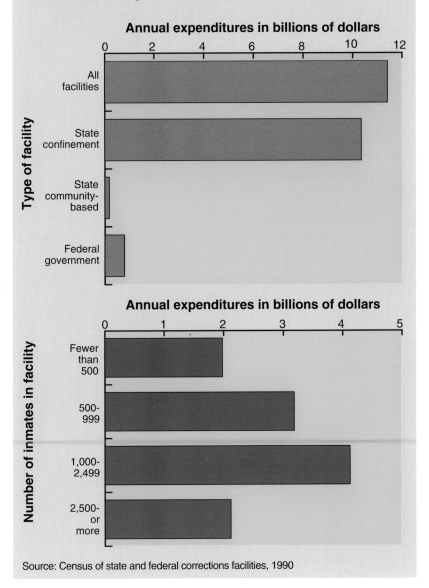

Expenditures for state and federal correctional facilities, July 1, 1989 to June 30, 1990

Source: Census of state and federal corrections facilities, 1990

programs, an extremely strict form of probation, is another alternative to prison. The convicted offender is required to report to a probation officer every day, hold a job, agree to random drug or alcohol tests, abide by a strict curfew, and be visited or called by phone at any hour of the day by a probation officer.

The state of Minnesota pioneered an experiment in 1980 to make sentencing more uniform while also reducing the number of nonviolent offenders going to prison. Based on a complicated sentencing guidelines grid, a judge evaluates each person to be sentenced, based on the severity of the crime and the person's criminal history. A specific score is determined that indicates the amount of time to be spent in prison.

Based on Minnesota's success, the state of Washington adopted a similar program. "We made the decision

An offender who is placed on probation must meet with a probation officer on a regular basis.

in Washington that prisons are made primarily to punish," said Chase Riveland, chief of Washington's correctional department. "We want longer terms for violent criminals and shorter terms for nonviolent property offenders."[7] The result? About 1,700 fewer people were incarcerated over the last couple of years with no noticeable effect on the crime rate.

"If we had been operating under the old law," claims Riveland, "I would have had to build at least three new facilities to hold those people, at a cost of $100 million and another $15 million a year operating costs."[8] With its surplus prison space, the state generates $27 million each year by renting cells to the federal government.

Compartmentalization is another prison alternative with many backers. This program places offenders with drug or alcohol problems, sex offenders, gambling addicts, or others with treatable conditions into specialized treatment centers staffed by trained counselors. Many such "halfway houses" now exist to treat the cause of the problem rather than to punish the offender. The major obstacle encountered by halfway houses is resistance by neighborhood groups who oppose having them located in their communities.

Alternatives to imprisonment are usually not popular with the general public. The familiar accusations of pampering and coddling are often voiced by a crime-weary public. Judges are understandably nervous, as well, over being perceived as soft on crime. When faced with the enormous sums required to continue building prisons at the present rate, however, many experts say taxpayers may modify their opposition to these alternatives.

Delancey Street in San Francisco, California, helps former convicts turn their lives around. It accepts no government funding and has no professional staff. Senior residents help new residents rehabilitate themselves.

10

SUCCESS STORIES

Many organizations and individuals actively help convicts and ex-convicts turn their lives around. The Fortune Society, Friends Outside, National Coalition for Jail Reform, Mennonite Central Committee, Prison Fellowship Ministers, and Prisoners' Rights Union are just a few.

Certainly one of the most remarkable and successful organizations is a San Francisco program called Delancey Street. It was founded in 1972 by Dr. Mimi Silbert, a former prison psychologist. More than 10,000 ex-convicts have undergone dramatic lifestyle changes under the tough-love approach of this residence.

As a teenager, Robert Rocha was a San Francisco street kid, using and selling drugs. His mother was in and out of jail for robbing banks. Since the age of eight, Rocha had been shuttled from one foster home to another. While still a juvenile, he had been arrested and charged with 27 holdups. By age 19, he was serving time in San Quentin.

"I'd lost touch with everything," Rocha says, "and

***Dr. Mimi Silbert, founder
of Delancey Street***

had no belief in myself. No hope. No trust in nothing
or nobody. I wanted to go to prison because that's
where I could be somebody."[1]

Now, at 30, Rocha is a well-groomed young man
who carries himself with quiet pride. Since entering
the Delancey Street program, he has learned eight construction trades and takes college courses in criminology. He tutors ex-convicts in geometry to help them
earn high school diplomas. He transformed his life on
every level—not in some magical way, but through Delancey Street's painstaking, step-by-step program.

The founder and guiding force behind Delancey
Street, Dr. Mimi Silbert, weighs less than 100 pounds
but stands toe-to-toe with the meanest and toughest ex-
felons society has to offer. When the group was building its new complex on the waterfront, Silbert

challenged Robert Rocha and the other Delancey Street residents when they felt like giving up. "You want to quit!" she chided them. "That's what you've *always* done—given up every time things got difficult! I know you're hammering away and thinking it isn't worth it, but you're hammering away at your lives!"[2]

Delancey Street is not an easy program, particularly for men and women who have never practiced self-discipline. Alcohol and drugs are forbidden, as is threatening—let alone committing—violence. In two decades a violent incident has never occurred. The few residents who did make threats were told to leave. Newcomers to Delancey Street are assigned maintenance chores at the bottom rung of the ladder. A drug addict who wakes up in the lobby is given a broom to push and told: "Now you're no longer an addict. Why? Because we don't allow drugs in here."

Delancey Street began when an ex-convict approached Dr. Silbert in 1971. He was interested in creating a rehabilitation program run for and by ex-cons. The program is totally self-sufficient, with no outside funding. Each resident must develop at least three marketable skills and earn a high school diploma. Residents follow strict rules of behavior and are self-governing.

The name Delancey Street was taken from the well-known New York City street that attracted immigrants at the turn of the century. Dr. Silbert was raised in a similar immigrant area of Boston and recalls the spirit of shared struggle that characterized such neighborhoods.

"I've duplicated here what worked in that neighborhood, where everybody looked out for everybody else as we struggled upward. It was like holding hands while climbing a mountain. Together we rise or together we fall. And that's what happens here every day."[3]

Delancey Street started out with four drug addicts living in a San Francisco apartment. Now it houses 500 residents at its new headquarters at the Embarcadero Triangle. Residents built the new structure, which is worth $30 million, almost entirely themselves. The complex contains 177 apartments, several meeting rooms, a movie theater, and a swimming pool. It also houses several businesses—a restaurant, print shop, picture-framing store, and a catering business. The various resident-operated ventures earn $3 million a year.

"When I interned as a prison psychologist," Dr. Silbert says, "it was clear that the system of punishment didn't work. Prisoners were given everything, all paid for by the taxpayers. They are responsible for nothing. And then we wonder why they're no different when they come out."[4]

Delancey Street graduates represent an extraordinary record of transformation. They include attorneys, businesspeople, technocrats, construction workers. The results are even more astonishing when the frightful histories of the residents are considered. They are people who had hit bottom.

"There's no way I'd go back to my old life," says Shirley LaMarr, a resident for nearly three years. "I went through the whole siege of drugs and prostitution, getting beat up and having guns drawn on me, getting raped and carried out on pills, you name it. I've robbed people, all kinds of stuff, and each year I'd feel more disgusted. I lived on the street, with my own space on the sidewalk. When I was arrested, I sent a

Some successful Delancey Street graduates

letter to Delancey Street. I was at the bottom, with a choice of coming here or going out to die."[5]

Robert Rocha recalls his hard-nosed attitude when he first arrived. "Nobody had ever cared about me, so why should I care about anyone else?"[6]

And he also remembers the moment when he began to care. "One of the guys was going to leave and I found myself shouting at him, trying to get him to stay. Some people told me, 'You're starting to care.' When I realized it was true—that I did care—I almost broke into tears."[7]

Gregory David Frye is one of the inmates on death row at the Mecklenburg Correctional Center in Boydton, Virginia. He has been in the custody of the state for all but his first 10 years of life.

CONCLUSION

Generalized descriptions of America's prisons are deceptive. The word *prison* barely applies to those minimum-security facilities with comfortably furnished rooms equipped with TVs and stereos, as well as parklike grounds where residents can picnic with visitors, polish their tennis skills, or sculpt their muscles on state-of-the-art Nautilus equipment. At the other extreme are the San Quentins, Atticas, and Leavenworths—"real joints."

Daily routines also vary radically from one prison to another. Lifer Charles Manson, for example, spends almost all his time in a 13-by-7-foot cell in the highest security wing of the state prison at Corcoran, California. His cell has no bars, because they are too risky. He contacts staff people through tiny holes. He has no physical contact with other prisoners, and he even exercises by himself.[1] In some of the so-called glamour slammers, on the other hand, the daily routine is as friendly as a Boy Scout camp.

Both extremes illustrate the divided (often opposing) opinions about solutions to the crime problem in the United States—punishment versus rehabilitation. One side contends that criminals did not show any sympathy toward their victims, so why should society show any compassion toward them? Without punishment that actually punishes, the "tough on crime" people say, what reason is there for criminals to lead honest lives?

Vengeful punishment, say their "soft on crime" opponents, will only result in making an already embittered underclass even more hostile. Providing humane prison conditions instead of merely caging lawbreakers like cattle is simple decency, according to this philosophy.

Underlying this swirling controversy is a basic assumption about the ability, or desire, of criminals to reform. Everyone acknowledges that some people appear

Charles Manson has no physical contact with other prisoners. His cell has no bars—only tiny holes.

to change for the better while in prison—but do they become better human beings *because* of their prison experience or *in spite* of it? As many parole board members will attest, determining which prisoners are reformed is a difficult task.

Prisons cannot solve the social ills that breed crime. Prisons cannot provide loving, nurturing parents, a decent standard of living, feelings of self-worth, or any of the other conditions generally needed to produce law-abiding human beings. It is unrealistic to expect a prison environment to miraculously transform sinners into saints.

Miracles do occur, however. While society is constantly reminded of its backsliders—the men and women who emerge from prison only to commit new crimes—those who succeed rarely make the headlines. But there are thousands of ex-offenders who have forged productive and successful lives from the most dismal backgrounds.

It is easy to become cynical about human nature when fed a daily diet of crime on television and in the newspapers. Many so-called criminals, however, are people whose lives have zigged when they should have zagged, basically decent people who have merely gotten caught up in a lifestyle dictated by drugs, alcohol, poverty, or neglect. As writer Ed Howe said: "There are no hopeless situations; there are only people who have grown hopeless about them."[2]

Realistically, of course, there are people who are either too dangerous or incorrigible to live in a free society. For them, we still have plenty of old-time penitentiaries—Attica, San Quentin, Leavenworth.

Resources to Contact

Academy of Criminal
  Justice Sciences
Northern Kentucky University
402 Numm Hall
Highland Heights, KY 41099-5998
Patricia DeLancey, Exec. Dir.
PH: (606) 572-5634

American Jail Association
2053 Day Rd., Ste. 100
Hagerstown, MD 21740
Stephen J. Ingley, Exec. Dir.
PH: (301) 790-3930

Center for Studies in Criminal Justice
University of Chicago Law School
1111 E. 60th St.
Chicago, IL 60637
Stephen J. Schulhofer, Dir.
PH: (312) 702-9493

Correctional Education Association
8025 Laurel Lakes Ct.
Laurel, MD 20707
Dr. Stephen J. Steurer, Exec. Dir.
PH: (301) 490-1440

Fortune Society
39 W. 19th St., 7th Fl.
New York, NY 10011
JoAnne Page, Exec. Dir.
PH: (212) 206-7070

Friends Outside
3031 Tischway, Ste. 507
San Jose, CA 95128
Judy Evans, Exec. Dir.
PH: (408) 985-8807

Guardian Angels
982 E. 89th St.
Brooklyn, NY 11236
Curtis Sliwa, Founder
PH: (212) 420-1324
FX: (212) 786-4048

International Association of
  Correctional Officers
1333 S. Wabash
Box 53
Chicago, IL 60605
PH: (312) 996-5401
FX: (312) 413-0458

International Prisoners
  Aid Association
University of Louisville
Dept. of Sociology
Louisville, KY 40292
Dr. Badr-El-Din Ali, Exec. Dir.
PH: (502) 588-6836

John Howard Association
67 E. Madison, Ste. 1416
Chicago, IL 60603
Michael J. Mahoney, Pres.
PH: (312) 263-1901

Prison Fellowship Ministries
P.O. Box 17500
Washington, D.C. 20041
Thomas Pratt, Pres.
PH: (703) 478-0100

Vera Institute of Justice
377 Broadway, 11th Fl.
New York, NY 10013
Michael E. Smith, Dir.
PH: (212) 334-1300

WETIP, Inc.
P.O. Box 1296
Rancho Cucamonga, CA 91729
Bill Brownell, Dir.
PH: (714) 987-5005
FX: (714) 987-2477

Women's Prison Association
110-2nd Ave.
New York, NY 10003
Ann L. Jacobs, Exec. Dir.
PH: (212) 334-1300

Endnotes

INTRODUCTION

[1] Abbott, Jack Henry, "Prisons Create a Criminal Personality," excerpted from *In the Belly of the Beast* (New York, Random House, 1981) in *America's Prisons*, (St. Paul, Minn., Greenhaven Press, 1985), Bonnie Szumski, Ed., 53.

[2] "Chronicles," *Time*, Nov. 7, 1994, 17.

[3] "Substance Abuse: The Nation's Number One Health Problem," Institute for Health Policy, Brandeis University, Oct. 1993.

[4] Holmes, Steven A., *New York Times,* reprinted in the Minneapolis *Star Tribune*, Nov. 18, 1994.

[5] Bureau of Justice Statistics Census, 1990, (Wash., D.C., U.S. Department of Justice), 18.

[6] Pierce, Neal R., *St. Paul Pioneer Press*, Jan. 14, 1992.

[7] Methvin, Eugene H., *Reader's Digest*, Nov. 1990, 70.

CHAPTER 1. FROM DUNGEONS TO PENITENTIARIES

[1] Menninger, Karl, *Crime of Punishment* (New York: The Viking Press, 1968), 192.

[2] Ibid., 195.

[3] *World Book* Encyclopedia, 1993 ed., s. v. "penal colonies."

[4] Silberman, Charles E., *Criminal Violence, Criminal Justice* (New York: Random House, 1978), 372.

[5] Weiss, Ann E., *Prisons: A System in Trouble* (Hillside, N.J.: Enslow Publishers, Inc., 1988), 28.

[6] Newman, Graeme R., "Prisons Should Be Dehumanizing," excerpted in *America's Prisons* (St. Paul, Minn.: Greenhaven Press, 1985), Bonnie Szumski, ed., 80.

[7] Holmes, Steven A., *New York Times,* reprinted in the Minneapolis *Star Tribune,* Nov. 13, 1994.

[8] Bureau of Justice Statistics, "Prisons and Prisoners in the United States" (Washington, D.C.: U.S. Department of Justice, 1992), 9.

[9] *Encyclopedia of Crime and Justice*, Vol. 3 (New York: The Free Press, 1983), 1197.

[10] *New York Times,* reprinted in the Minneapolis *Star Tribune,* March 27, 1995.

CHAPTER 2. TYPES OF PRISONS

[1] Bureau of Justice Statistics, "Census of State and Federal Correctional Facilities" (Washington, D.C.: U.S. Department of Justice, 1990), 1.

[2] Ibid., 20.

[3] Bureau of Justice Statistics, "Prisons and Prisoners in the United States" (Washington, D.C.: U.S. Department of Justice, 1992), 3.

CHAPTER 3. WHO GOES TO PRISON?

[1] Meltzer, Milton, *Crime in America* (New York: Morrow Junior Books, 1990), 50.

[2] Stevenson, Richard, *New York Times*, reprinted in the Minneapolis *Star Tribune*, Apr. 11, 1992.

[3] Bureau of Justice Statistics, "Prisoners in 1993" (Washington, D.C.: U.S. Department of Justice, June 1994), 9.

[4] Marcus, Ruth, "Race and the Scales of Justice," *Washington Post,* reprinted in the Minneapolis *Star Tribune*, May 13, 1992.

[5] Ibid.

[6] Ibid.

[7] Ibid.

[8] Ibid.

[9] Ibid.

[10] *New Yorker,* "The Talk of the Town," Apr. 13, 1992, 27.

[11] Ibid.

[12] Pierce, Neal R., *St. Paul Pioneer Press,* Jan. 14, 1992.

[13] Langan, Patrick A., "America's Soaring Prison Population," *Science,* Mar. 29, 1991, 1568.

[14] Bureau of Justice Statistics, "Prisoners in 1993" (Washington, D.C.: U.S. Dept. of Justice, June 1994), 1.

CHAPTER 4. INSIDE THE BIG HOUSE

[1] Bureau of Justice Statistics, "Census of State and Federal Correctional Facilities, 1990" (Washington, D.C.: U.S. Department of Justice, 1992), 12.

[2] *US. News & World Report,* "Factories Behind Bars," Jan. 6, 1992, 30.

[3] Greene, Richard, "Who's Punishing Whom?" *Forbes,* Mar. 21, 1988, 132.

[4] Miller, Mark, "When Convicts Get Competitive," *Newsweek,* Aug. 20, 1990, 44.

[5] "Factories Behind Bars," *U.S. News & World Report,* Jan. 6, 1992, 30.

[6] McDowell, Edwin, "Inmates Tout State's Assets On Tourist Line," *New York Times*, Nov. 24, 1991, 1.

[7] Ibid., 1.

[8] Lacey, Carol, "Journey of Hope," *St. Paul Pioneer Press*, Dec. 15, 1991.

[9] Ibid., 5F.

[10] Ticer, Scott, "The Search for Ways to Break out of the Prison Crisis," *Business Week,* May 8, 1989, 80.

CHAPTER 5. PRISON VIOLENCE

[1] Bureau of Justice Statistics, "Prisoners in 1993" (Washington, D.C.: U.S. Department of Justice, June 1994), 4.

[2] Dawson, Jim, Minneapolis *Star Tribune*, Feb. 18, 1995.

[3] Ibid., 54.

[4] Lacey, Carol, "Journey of Hope," Minneapolis *Star Tribune*, Dec. 15, 1991.

[5] *Corrections Compendium*, June 1994, 9.

[6] Anderson, 431.

[7] Scripps Howard News Service, reprinted in the Minneapolis *Star Tribune,* March 24, 1992.

[8] Ibid.

[9] Ibid.

[10] Ibid.

[11] Anderson, 432.

[12] Ibid., 431.

[13] Ibid., 431.

[14] Logan, Andy, "Peacekeepers," *New Yorker*, Sept. 10, 1990, 105.

[15] Ibid.

[16] Rochman, Sue, "Alternatives to Prison Violence," *Corrections Compendium*, June 1991, 6.

[17] Ibid., 8.

[18] Ibid., 8.

CHAPTER 6. WOMEN IN PRISON

[1] Bureau of Justice Statistics, "Prisoners in 1993" (Washington, D.C.: U.S. Department of Justice, June 1994), 4.

[2] Bureau of Justice Statistics (Washington, D.C.: U.S. Department of Justice, 1991).

[3] Bureau of Justice Statistics, "Women in Prison" (Washington, D. C.: U.S. Department of Justice, March 1994), 7.

[4] Ibid., 2.

[5] Ibid., 6.

[6] Butterfield, Fox, "Studies Find a Link to Criminality," *New York Times*, Jan. 30, 1992.

[7] Bureau of Justice Statistics, "Women in Prison," (Washington, D.C.: U.S. Department of Justice, March 1994), 5.

[8] Ibid., 7.

[9] Prince, Pat, "Actors Have Script, But Play's Scenes All Too Familiar," Minneapolis *Star Tribune*, Apr. 9, 1992.

[10] Ibid.

CHAPTER 7. JUVENILE LOCKUPS

[1] Bauer, Joseph, ed., "Letters to You from Teenagers in Jail," excerpted in *Seventeen*, Aug. 1991.

[2] Parent, Dale G., "Conditions of Confinement," *Juvenile Justice*, Office of Juvenile Justice and Delinquency Prevention (Washington, D.C.: U.S. Department of Justice, Spring/Summer 1993), 2.

[3] Allen-Hagen, Barbara, "Children in Custody," Office of Juvenile Justice and Delinquency Prevention (Washington, D.C.: U.S. Department of Justice, Oct. 1988), 3.

[4] Diaz, Kevin, "Juvenile or Adult?" Minneapolis *Star Tribune*, Apr. 20, 1992.

[5] Ibid.

[6] Toufexis, Anastasia, "Our Violent Kids," *Time*, June 12, 1989, 57.

[7] Raspberry, William, "Deterring Apprentices in Crime," *Washington Post,* reprinted in the Minneapolis *Star Tribune*, Apr. 24, 1992.

[8] Ibid.

[9] Slott, Irving (Interviewer), Office of Juvenile Justice and Delinquency Prevention (Washington D.C.: U.S. Department of Justice, Spring/Summer 1993), 16.

[10] Basten, Patricia Lopez, "Juvenile Rehabilitation—A Myth?" Minneapolis *Star Tribune*, Feb. 16, 1995.

CHAPTER 8. AIDS—A CORRECTIONAL TIME BOMB

[1] Center for Disease Control, "HIV/AIDS Surveillance Report," 1994: 5 (no. 4), 17–18.

[2] Hammett, Theodore M. and Saira Moini of Abt Associates, Inc., AIDS Bulletin, "Update on AIDS in Prisons and Jails" (Washington, D.C., U.S. Department of Justice), Sept. 1990, 2.

[3] Harlow, Carline Wolf, Bureau of Justice Statistics, "HIV in U.S. Prisons and Jails" (Wash., D.C., Department of Justice), Sept. 1993, 6.

[4] Ibid., 2–4.

[5] Hammett and Moini, 10.

CHAPTER 9. ALTERNATIVES TO PRISON

[1] Cronin, Mary, "Gilded Cages," *Time*, May 25, 1992, 52.

[2] Lacayo, Richard, "Our Bulging Prisons," *Time*, May 29, 1989, 29.

[3] Sullivan, Robert E. Jr., "Reach Out and Guard Someone: Using Phones and Bracelets to Reduce Prison Overcrowding," *Rolling Stone*, Nov. 29, 1990, 51.

[4] Ibid.
[5] Ibid.
[6] Ibid.
[7] Greene, Richard, "Who's Punishing Whom?" *Forbes*, Mar. 21, 1988, 136.
[8] Ibid.

CHAPTER 10. SUCCESS STORIES

[1] Whittemore, Hank, "Hitting Bottom Can Be the Beginning," *Parade,* Mar. 15, 1992, 4.
[2] Ibid., 5.
[3] Ibid., 6.
[4] Ibid.
[5] Ibid., 5.
[6] Ibid.
[7] Ibid.

CONCLUSION

[1] Kaplan, David A., "Silence of the Wolves," *Newsweek*, Feb. 3, 1992, 51.
[2] Howe, Ed, *20,000 Quips & Quotes* (Garden City, N.Y.: Doubleday & Company, Inc., 1968), 394.

Glossary

alternative sentence: any one of a variety of community-based punishments imposed instead of prison, such as a halfway house, probation, electronic home monitoring, community service

anonymity: the state or quality of being unnamed or unidentified

arson: maliciously setting fire to a building or property, often for the purpose of collecting insurance

bail: money the accused leaves with the court as a pledge that he or she will appear in court on the assigned day. The money is forfeited if the person does not appear in court.

criminologist: a person who has studied crime and criminals; a professional, or expert, who specializes in the field of crime

delinquent: a person who violates the law

electronic home monitoring: an electronic device attached to a convicted person's ankle for the purpose of keeping track of his or her movements; a form of home incarceration, also known as home arrest

felony: any crime punishable by death or confinement for more than one year in prison. All serious crimes are felonies.

halfway house: a house where a group of people live for the purpose of treatment or as an alternative to imprisonment, usually under a court order

homicide: killing of one person by another; murder or manslaughter.

incarceration: imprisonment or confinement in a correctional facility

mandatory sentence: a law requiring a minimum number of years in prison for certain offenses; also known as "mandatory minimums."

misdemeanor: any minor offense, usually punishable by a fine or less than one year in jail; generally served in a local jail or workhouse.

parole: the release of a prisoner after serving a portion of his or her sentence in prison. Parole can be revoked by a parole officer—and the parolee returned to prison—if any of the conditions of parole are violated.

probation: similar to parole, except the entire sentence is served in the community under the supervision of a probation officer. No imprisonment is required as long as the probationer complies with the rules of probation. If probation is revoked, the entire sentence must be served in prison.

prosecutor: the attorney who represents the government when a person is charged with a crime; also known as the prosecuting attorney

recidivism: refers to repeated convictions after having served time in prison. Repeat offenders are recidivists.

rehabilitation: the process by which a person who has served time in prison goes on to become a law-abiding citizen

restitution: financial payment made by criminals to the victims of their crimes

Bibliography

Books

Abbott, Jack Henry. *In the Belly of the Beast.* New York: Random House, 1981.

Bernards, Neal, and Bonnie Szumski. *Prisons.* San Diego: Greenhaven Press, Inc., 1990.

Clark, Phyllis Elperin, and Robert Lehrman. *Doing Time.* New York: Hastings House, 1980.

Encyclopedia of Crime and Justice. Vol. 3. New York: The Free Press, 1983.

Howe, Ed. *20,000 Quips & Quotes.* Garden City, NY: Doubleday & Company, Inc., 1968.

Meltzer, Milton. *Crime in America.* New York: Morrow Junior Books, 1990.

Menninger, Karl. *Crime of Punishment.* New York: Viking Press, 1968.

Silberman, Charles E. *Criminal Violence, Criminal Justice.* New York: Random House, 1978.

Szumski, Bonnie, Ed. *America's Prisons.* St. Paul, MN: Greenhaven Press, 1985.

Warburton, Lois. *Prisons.* San Diego: Lucent Books, Inc., 1993.

Weiss, Ann E. *Prisons: A System in Trouble.* Hillside, NJ: Enslow Publishers, Inc., 1988.

World Book Encyclopedia. Vol. 15, "Penal Colonies." Chicago: Field Enterprises Educational Corp., 1973.

Magazines/Articles

Allen-Hagen, Barbara. "Children in Custody." Office of Juvenile Justice and Delinquency Prevention , U.S. Dept. of Justice, Oct. 1988, 3.

Anderson, George M. "Prison Violence: Victims Behind Bars." *America*, Nov. 26, 1988, 431–432.

Bauer, Joseph, Ed. "Letters to You from Teenagers in Jail." *Seventeen*, Aug. 1991, 238–239.

Bureau of Justice Statistics. "Census." U.S. Dept of Justice, 1990, 18. "Census of State and Federal Correctional Facilities," 1992, 12. "Census of State and Federal Correctional Facilities," 1990, 1–20. "HIV in U.S. Prisons and Jails," Sept. 1993, 2–3–4–6. "Prisoners in 1993," June 1994, 1–4. "Prisons and Prisoners in the United States," 1992, 3–9. "Women in Prison," March 1994, 2–5/6–7.

Center for Disease Control, "Surveillance Report—HIV/AIDS." Washington, D.C.: U.S. Dept. of Health and Human Services, Aug. 1994, 5.

Cronin, Mary. "Gilded Cages." *Time*, May 25, 1992, 52.

Davis, Su Perk. *Corrections Compendium*, June 1991, 9.

"Factories Behind Bars." *U.S. News & World Report,* Jan. 6, 1992, 30.

Greene, Richard. "Who's Punishing Whom?" *Forbes*, March 21, 1988, 132–136.

Hammett, Theodore M., and Saira Moini, Abt. Associates, Inc., "Update on AIDS in Prisons and Jails," *AIDS Bulletin.* Washington, D.C.: U.S. Dept. of Justice, Sept. 1990, 2–10.

Kantrowitz, Barbara, and Karen Springer. "Hooking Up at the Big House." *Time*, June 1, 1992, 65.

Kaplan, David A. "Silence of the Wolves." *Newsweek*, Feb. 3, 1992, 51.

Lacayo, Richard. "Our Bulging Prisons." *Time*, May 29, 1989, 29.

Langan, Patrick A. "America's Soaring Prison Population." *Science*, March 29, 1991, 1568.

Logan, Andy. "Peacekeepers." *New Yorker*, Sept. 10, 1990, 105.

Methvin, Eugene H. *Reader's Digest*, Nov. 1990, 70.

Miller, Mark. "When Convicts Get Competitive." *Newsweek*, Aug. 20, 1990, 44.

Parent, Dale G. "Conditions of Confinement." *Juvenile Justice.* Office of Juvenile Justice and Delinquency Prevention. Washington, D.C.: U.S. Dept. of Justice, Spring/Summer 1993, 2.

Rochman, Sue. "Alternatives to Prison Violence." *Corrections Compendium*, June 1991, 6–8.

Slott, Irving (Interview). *Juvenile Justice and Delinquency Prevention.* Washington, D.C.: U.S. Dept. of Justice, Spring/Summer 1993, 16.

Sullivan, Robert E. Jr. "Reach Out and Guard Someone: Using Phones and Bracelets to Reduce Prison Overcrowding." *Rolling Stone*, Nov. 29, 1990, 51.

"The Talk of the Town." *New Yorker.* April 13, 1992, 27.

Ticer, Scott. "The Search for Ways to Break Out of Prison Crisis." *Business Week*, May 8, 1989, 80.

Toufexis, Anastasia. "Our Violent Kids." *Time*, June 12, 1989, 52–57.

Whittemore, Hank. "Hitting Bottom Can Be the Beginning." *Parade,* March 15, 1992, 46.

Index

ABOUT THE AUTHOR

Andy Hjelmeland writes about prisons with special insight. Many years of his youth and early adulthood were spent in correctional facilities—reform schools, work farms, and city and county lockups. "I can't even estimate the number of times I've been arrested," he said.

He began writing in prison and has been published in *Newsweek, Sports Illustrated, The Nation, Minneapolis-St. Paul Magazine,* the Minneapolis *Star Tribune,* and other publications. He has also published two books for young people: *Drinking and Driving* and *Kids in Jail.* The latter was selected by the New York Public Library as one of the Best Books for the Teen Age.

Hjelmeland lives in Minneapolis and works at a Twin Cities television station in addition to doing freelance writing.

PHOTO ACKNOWLEDGMENTS

AP/Wide World, 23, 28, 53; Bettmann Archive, 9, 42; California Department of Corrections, 33, 58, 76, 82, 86, 101; the Chemung County Historical Society, Elmira, New York, 20; Delancey Street Foundation, 92, 95; M. Bryan Ginsburg, 26; Hollywood Book and Poster, 50; Jim Hubbard, 70; © Ed Kashi, cover, 14, 46, 54, 55, 66, 71; Library of Congress, 17; © Bob Swansen, 90; National Cancer Institute, 81; Reuters/Bettmann, 19, 31; Mark Richards, 40; Nancy Smedstad, IPS, 10; UPI/Bettmann, 6, 12, 29, 37, 47, 64, 96, 98; Dennis Wolf, 73, 88.